SUDDEN DEATH

SUDDEN DEATH

The Incredible Saga
of the 1986 Swift Current Broncos

Leesa Culp | *Gregg Drinnan* | *Bob Wilkie*

DUNDURN
TORONTO

Project Editor: Cheryl Hawley
Editor: Jenny Govier
Design: Courtney Horner
Printer: Webcom

Library and Archives Canada Cataloguing in Publication

Culp, Leesa
    Sudden death : the incredible saga of the 1986 Swift Current
Broncos / by Leesa Culp, Gregg Drinnan, and Bob Wilkie ; foreword
by Brian Costello.

Issued also in electronic formats.
ISBN 978-1-4597-0544-9

    1. Swift Current Broncos (Hockey team). 2. Traffic accidents--
Saskatchewan--Swift Current. 3. Hockey players--Saskatchewan--
Swift Current. 4. Hockey players--Death. 5. Memorial Cup (Hockey)
(1989 : Saskatoon, Sask.). I. Drinnan, Gregg II. Wilkie, Bob, 1969-
III. Title.

GV848.S94C84 2012   796.962'620971243   C2012-904464-4

1   2   3   4   5   16   15   14   13   12

Conseil des Arts   Canada Council   **Canadä**   **ONTARIO ARTS COUNCIL**
du Canada   for the Arts   **CONSEIL DES ARTS DE L'ONTARIO**

We acknowledge the support of the **Canada Council for the Arts** and the **Ontario Arts Council** for our publishing program. We also acknowledge the financial support of the **Government of Canada** through the **Canada Book Fund** and **Livres Canada Books,** and the **Government of Ontario** through the **Ontario Book Publishing Tax Credit** and the **Ontario Media Development Corporation.**

Printed and bound in Canada.

Visit us at
Dundurn.com
Definingcanada.ca
@dundurnpress
Facebook.com/dundurnpress

Dundurn	Gazelle Book Services Limited	Dundurn
3 Church Street, Suite 500	White Cross Mills	2250 Military Road
Toronto, Ontario, Canada	High Town, Lancaster, England	Tonawanda, NY
M5E 1M2	LA1 4XS	U.S.A. 14150

I believe that somehow this tragedy has made us all stronger. Our lives will always be connected. I thank my friends whom I lost that day: Trent Kresse, Scotty Kruger, Chris Mantyka, and Brent Ruff. Without you guys in my life, I don't know where I would have ended up. Thanks, guys ... I love you very much. This book is dedicated to your memory.

Bob Wilkie
Calgary, Alberta
January 2012

I'd like to thank my daughter Maggie and my son Carter, who have had to deal with "not so good" cooking, "not so clean" clothes, and "Not now ... I'm working on the book again," way too much. You are the joy in my life and I thank you for hanging in there when I needed some extra time for me. And, of course, I want to thank my extraordinarily talented husband, Bill, who, with Maggie and Carter, completes me. You have been with me for over twenty-seven years and your encouragement and belief in my ability to reach my goals is infectious and contributes so much to my determination. I dedicate this book to you.

Leesa Culp
Beamsville, Ontario
January 2012

CONTENTS

Foreword

Eight hours after the fact, in the wee hours of the morning, the accident site looked serene. Bathed in snowy darkness, only the bouncing lights from passing transport trucks showed the battle scars left from the previous afternoon.

Who would have believed that a routine Western Hockey League road trip to Regina on December 30, 1986, would turn into a nightmare for the Swift Current Broncos and the tightly knit rural Saskatchewan community of 16,000 citizens?

Four players died that afternoon when the team bus veered off the Trans-Canada Highway a few kilometres east of Swift Current, catapulted off an approach road, and landed on its side.

Why that time? Why that place?

Eight hours later, not much remained at the site. The wreckage of the bus had been hauled away. A couple of centimetres of new-fallen snow masked the tire tracks, the footprints, and the confusion.

As I walked through the wild oats in the ditch, I came across a hockey stick. It wasn't far from where the bodies of Scotty Kruger and Trent Kresse had been found. Thirty metres ahead was the bruised stretch of ditch where the bus had come to rest. This was where the crushed bodies of Brent Ruff and Chris Mantyka had been discovered.

I didn't need to see more. I picked up the hockey stick, put it in my car, drove home to my basement rental pad, and spent the night sitting alone in a chair in the dark.

What had happened?

The next day, we didn't know why it happened. And now, more than twenty-five years later, we still don't know why it happened to those people at that time in that place. This book isn't about trying to find answers to those questions. That's a fruitless exercise.

Weather reports told us there was freezing rain in that location that afternoon. Eyewitness accounts told us the Broncos' bus had just gone over a railway overpass when it caught a patch of ice, which led to its deadly slide off the road. Police reports told us the impact of the bus with the approach road led to the vehicle becoming airborne and landing on its right side.

A coroner's report told us the four victims died from spinal injuries when they were either thrown from the bus or crushed beneath it.

Those facts help us deal with the acceptance part of the equation, but do nothing for our quest to seek a greater understanding of why certain events unfold at certain times and in certain places.

Swift Current players Ryan McGill and Dan Lambert hadn't missed a game all season. But on December 30, McGill was sick and Lambert was at an under-seventeen game in another city. Fate kept them off the bus that day.

Trainer Gordie Hahn wasn't on the bus because he accompanied Lambert to his game. Hahn has since struggled with personal demons as he tries to understand why he was taken away from the group of players he was paid to take care of. Why that particular game?

In Hahn's place, Doug Leavins was filling in as trainer for one game. On December 30, Leavins became a hero as he hobbled around with a broken pelvic bone and performed CPR in a vain attempt to revive Kruger and Kresse. Why was he called upon that day?

Free-agent goaltender Artie Feher had joined the Broncos the day before the accident. He survived the crash, removed himself from the team, and went home to Prince Albert. What forces conspired to land him with the Broncos for just those forty-eight hours?

Circumstance puts each of us in a certain time and place on a constant basis. And 99.9 percent of the time, we don't ask why.

For Leesa Culp, then twenty-one years of age, that day put her in the exhaust fumes of the out-of-control Broncos bus. An uneasy passenger in an eastbound transport truck, Culp was at a crossroads in her life when she witnessed the accident.

Culp was the first person to arrive at the sides of Kresse and Kruger. Just seconds after the accident, she held Kresse's hand and watched the life drain from his face. Before she even got a chance to digest what was happening, she was back in the truck and eastbound again.

Culp moved on literally and metaphorically. She put on blinders and refused to deal with the personal baggage of the accident. She got married, started a career, began raising a family. It took her twenty years to start asking questions, and when she did, she didn't stop. Why had fate led her to that particular place at that particular time? She is the driving force behind this book.

Culp tracked me down in the autumn of 2007. The Internet had led her to old stories about the accident and prompted her to find the *Swift Current Sun* reporter who had been on that bus. She contacted me at my office at *The Hockey News* in Toronto and politely uncorked a barrage of questions. The most pressing question was, "Tell me about the dying boy whose hand I held. I don't even know his name."

The flood of emotions that came from Culp during that conversation got me thinking about people and time and place again.

Graham James, the Broncos' general manager and head coach, had intended to return sixteen-year-old Brent Ruff to the midget ranks that season. But it was Ruff's insistent and passionate plea to remain with the Broncos during their one-on-one meeting that changed James's mind.

James was a strong advocate of a skill-and-finesse game above all else. But it was Chris Mantyka's heart, character, and inner will that earned the enforcer a job on a team full of speed and dazzle.

Inseparable off the ice, Scott Kruger and Trent Kresse died side by side when thrown from the bus. In a scene full of horror and grief, one supposes that was only fitting.

Other circumstances led the other players and passengers to be part of that bus journey on that day. And you'll get a glimpse of them in the pages to come.

For me, Swift Current was a two-year stop on my career in hockey journalism. As much as I would like to trade that one tragic day for a dozen of my second-worst days, I look back fondly on my experiences in Speedy Creek.

My biggest post-accident struggle was dealing with not having done my part to alter the time-place thread.

As Kresse boarded the bus that afternoon, he smiled and sat next to me. I sat in my regular spot behind Dave Archibald, the driver. As we pulled out of town, we talked about Christmas holidays, family, and feasting. Just as I asked about his ice-fishing exploits in Kindersley, he excused himself. A card game with Kruger, Ruff, and Mantyka awaited in the back seat. There would be time to talk later.

There's no sense in trying to understand the time-place continuum.

In the years since the accident, my career has taken me to hundreds of hockey games in various outposts. The cars I have driven have come and gone, but with me at all times, pressed tightly between the front seats, is that hockey stick, the one I found at the accident site. It may have belonged to Kresse, it may not have. All that matters is that it is my safety net and my link to time, place, and circumstance.

Brian Costello
Senior Special Editions Editor
The Hockey News
January 2012

CHAPTER 1

The Road Back

Twenty years.

That's how long it had been since Sheldon Kennedy, Peter Soberlak, and Bob Wilkie had been together like this. Twenty years.

Oh, two of them may have bumped into each other on occasion, perhaps while chasing a loose puck into a corner of a rink in Adirondack, New York, or the arena in Sydney on Cape Breton Island. Perhaps they had even gone out for a beer or two after one of those games.

But it had been twenty years since the three of them had been together like this. Just the three of them. Nobody else. Riding down the highway of life.

The last time they were together in a situation where they could "shoot the poop," as one of them would put it, the Tiananmen Square protests were in the headlines and Mikhail Gorbachev was visiting China, the first time a Soviet leader had done that in a long, long time.

But now it was August 2009 and things were different. Each had recently turned forty years of age. They all were married or had been married or were in a relationship. All were proud fathers. To say a lot of water had gone under the bridge would be to understate things in a big, big way.

They had agreed to meet in a Calgary subdivision, at the home of Wilkie's parents. Wilkie had arrived early, from the Hershey, Pennsylvania, area, in order to spend a day or two with his family. Soberlak flew in from Kamloops, British Columbia, and was met by Wilkie at the Calgary airport.

"As I found myself driving to the airport to pick up Sober, I was nervous," Wilkie admits. "What was it going to be like? How would it be with the three of us together? What would we talk about?

"But I saw Sober sitting on the curb waiting for me and all of the questions were gone immediately. None of it mattered; it was just us guys, soul brothers together again. After a big hug and some laughs, we were on our way."

Wilkie and Soberlak visited around the Wilkie home and enjoyed a barbecue as they waited for Kennedy to pick them up.

"While we were having lunch we talked about all of the things we had done over the last twenty years," Wilkie remembers. "It was like we hadn't seen each other in a week rather than twenty years. When you connect like we did and went through what we did, what we accomplished together, there is a soul connection, and Peter is one of those guys I am blessed to have that connection with."

When Kennedy arrived, they clambered into his truck and headed east. Their destination was Swift Current, Saskatchewan, the scene of the triumphs and tragedies that had done so much to shape the men they had become.

Kennedy, Soberlak, and Wilkie had been born within four months of each other in 1969. They were teammates on the Western Hockey League's Swift Current Broncos in the late 1980s. Calling them teammates really doesn't do justice to their relationship, though, because not many teammates experience what they did.

They had been on their team bus when it crashed, killing four teammates, just east of Swift Current on December 30, 1986.

They had been teammates on May 13, 1989, when the Broncos, in just the second season after the bus accident, took ownership of the entire hockey world by winning the Memorial Cup.

And those Broncos teams had been under the thumb of Graham James, the franchise's general manager and head coach, who, as we would come to learn in time, was sexually assaulting Kennedy and at least one other player during the team's run.

Now Kennedy, Soberlak, and Wilkie were in the cab of a truck headed for Swift Current, where a weekend reunion would celebrate the winning of the Memorial Cup title in Saskatoon more than twenty years earlier.

Wilkie had arrived in Calgary with his wife, Mikey, and children, Sadie and Cy, to visit his parents. Mikey and the kids had then returned home, and Wilkie, at the invitation of Hockey Alberta, had driven to Camrose to speak at a symposium.

It was on the drive to Camrose when the scope of the reunion — and exactly what it would mean for these three men to return to Swift Current — began to sink in.

"The reunion was only a couple of days away and I found myself a little scared and nervous," Wilkie admits. "I was going to see people I hadn't seen in twenty years. So much happened when we were together and few of us had talked about any of it … unfinished business, I guess you could call it."

Once the three were together again, though, it was like they had never been apart.

"Sheldon picked us up in his truck," a grinning Soberlak says, "and we hit the long, flat road and never shut up for five hours."

"We just started shooting the poop right off the hop," Kennedy recalls. "Wilks is Mr. Happy-Go-Lucky … a jolly, laid-back kind of dude. Peter and I … our aspirations were things other than hockey.

"There was some of the hockey talk, but there was a lot of talk about Swift and some of the stuff that went on. There were some pretty deep conversations and we needed conversation.

"And we had a lot of laughs."

Still, the chatter and the laughs were overshadowed by the dark side of what they had experienced.

"As we headed out of town," Wilkie says, "the three of us were like we were eighteen again. Only now we were talking about kids, marriage, and careers. That in itself made us all laugh."

As Swift Current drew closer, the tone of the conversation changed.

"We talked of all the good times," Wilkie explains, "and then it made a shift over to the dark side as we got closer and started talking about Graham, the owners … Sheldon started shedding some light on things we had no idea about.

"In his journey of pressing charges, Sheldon had hired a private investigator and learned things that made our skin crawl. Peter and I didn't know what to say, and for me personally it shed light on something that I had wondered about for the last twenty years."

Kennedy easily was the best known of the trio. An inordinately gifted hockey player, he had been born in Brandon, Manitoba, on June 15, 1969, and had grown up in places like Thompson and Elkhorn, two other Manitoba communities.

Kennedy was selected by the Detroit Red Wings in the fourth round, eightieth overall, of the 1988 National Hockey League draft. Always seen as something of a free spirit, a mustang, if you will, Kennedy never was able to find a professional home, and spent much of his time shuttling between the NHL and the American Hockey League.

For much of the early days of his professional career, he was seen as an enigma, a problem child who could be a solid player if only someone could figure him out and get through to him. As his career wore on, it became more and more obvious that he was a troubled young man. But it wasn't until the 1996–97 season that the pieces began to come together.

It was then, while he was nearing the end of his professional career, that Kennedy rocked the hockey world by claiming that he had been sexually abused by Graham James for a number of years.

Kennedy, who would tell his story in the book *Why I Didn't Say Anything: The Sheldon Kennedy Story*, now lives near Calgary and spends his life working toward eradicating abuse and bullying of any kind. Late in 2011, he appeared before a House of Commons justice and human rights committee to speak in support of a government crime bill.

"I believe that we need to toughen sentencing for child sex offences," he told the committee. "They just don't seem in line with the damage they leave in their wake. Not even close."

If children are being abused, Kennedy said, they need to know that if they come forward, justice will be served.

"To me the fundamental reason for change to these laws is simple," he continued. "We can't let these perpetrators walk freely among our youth organizations, our schools, our neighbourhoods, and our work places. Children need to feel safe and parents have to trust that the government is playing a role in protecting them.

"Criminals need to be held accountable and be dealt with consistently with clearly defined consequences. In my mind, child protection is paramount."

All this came from a guy who at one time would offer up more giggles than words when he was in an interview situation. At the time, of course, no one understood the pressures under which Kennedy simply was trying to survive.

Sheldon Kennedy had come a long way, and he was quickly becoming someone who was bound and determined to make a difference in his world.

Later, as October 2011 turned into November, the community of Neepawa, Manitoba, became embroiled in an ugly hazing scandal that involved its Manitoba Junior Hockey League franchise, the Natives. One player, a fifteen-year-old, had blown the whistle and was now being ostracized. Kennedy took it upon himself to contact the young player.

"Sheldon Kennedy gave him his personal cell phone [number] and said, 'Any time you want to talk to me about this just phone me, doesn't matter what time of day it is,'" the player's father said. "My son was going, 'Wow.'"

Kennedy said he had "just wanted to reach out to him and tell him I think he's doing the right thing. If I can be there to support and help in any way, I will be."

Soberlak flew into Calgary from Kamloops, where he is the chairman of Thompson Rivers University's department of athletics. He also was president of the Kamloops Sports Council, an organization that oversees a lot of amateur sports in the city.

Soberlak was born on May 12, 1969, in Trail, British Columbia, the home of the legendary Smoke Eaters. He played his minor hockey in

Kamloops, where he began the serious part of his hockey career with the WHL's Blazers under head coach Ken Hitchcock.

Early hockey memories are anything but happy ones for Soberlak, who says his first season — he was sixteen years of age — in Kamloops "was hell."

"It was horrible," he says. "The way I was treated by the coaching staff and the players...."

A highly skilled player with a sensitive side that ran contrary to what most, if not all, major junior hockey coaches demand from their players, Soberlak played in an era that was a whole lot different from the one that exists today. In fact, Soberlak admits he lived in fear of being hazed, something that happened to rookies with frightening regularity in the days when the law of the jungle governed the junior game.

Early in his seventeen-year-old season, Soberlak was traded to Swift Current and found himself on a line with Kennedy and future NHL superstar Joe Sakic.

"When I got traded, I got rejuvenated," Soberlak says. "I was playing on a line with Sheldon and Joe. But you know what? That was temporary; the damage was done. At seventeen, I was still in it, but after that I started to disconnect and distance myself from the love of the game.

Swift Current Broncos players Sheldon Kennedy (left), Joe Sakic, and Peter Soberlak.

Rod Steensland.

Bob Wilkie

"I had lost the love of the game during my sixteen-year-old year in Kamloops."

Soberlak was a superb physical specimen, at six foot three and two hundred pounds, and with a hockey stick in his hands he was a magician. Because of his size, hockey people assumed he would be a physical force on the ice. But that wasn't his game, and early in his third professional season, Soberlak shrugged his shoulders and walked away from hockey.

He had been a first-round selection in the 1987 NHL draft, taken twenty-first overall by the Edmonton Oilers. He never played a game in the NHL.

When Soberlak arrived at the airport in Calgary, he was met by Wilkie, who had grown up in Calgary. In fact, Wilkie began his major junior career with the WHL's Calgary Wranglers. A strong-skating offensive-type defenceman with good size — he would play professionally at six foot two and 215 pounds — Wilkie was always seen as something of a nonconformist. That, in fact, may have led to his being traded by Calgary general manager John Chapman to the Broncos just one game into the 1986–87 season.

Wilkie was a gifted puck-handler, something that Graham James treasured in a player. James would get more than a point per game out of Wilkie over two-plus seasons.

Wilkie, however, is one of those personalities who always seem to be searching for something — the meaning of life, perhaps — and, like Kennedy, he would spend most of his pro career wandering in hockey's hinterlands.

Like Kennedy, Wilkie was a draft pick of the Red Wings, taken in the second round, forty-first overall, in 1987, the same draft in which Soberlak was selected. (In fact, five Broncos were taken in that draft. Sakic was selected by the Quebec Nordiques with the fifteenth overall pick; defenceman Ryan McGill went twenty-ninth overall to the Chicago Blackhawks; and, defenceman Ian Herbers was selected by the Buffalo Sabres with the 180th pick.)

Wilkie's career would end up reading like a Hank Snow country tune — Adirondack, Detroit, Adirondack, Fort Wayne, Adirondack, Hershey, Philadelphia, Indianapolis, Hershey, Augsburg, Cincinnati, Fresno, Las Vegas, Fresno, Pensacola, and Anchorage — before he called it quits. For a few years after, he lived near Hershey working as an "attitude coach," consultant, and speaker.

Kennedy, Soberlak, and Wilkie hadn't been together like this, they agreed, since the late spring — actually, hockey playoffs going on forever the way they do, it was early summer — of 1989, when they were celebrating that improbable Memorial Cup championship.

"It was probably at the parade … after the parade," a laughing Kennedy would say twenty years later. "What was it, Peter? A three-week party."

To which Soberlak replied, "I remember playing golf in my bare feet about the third day. I was real sick and missed the banquet."

Yes, those Broncos knew how to throw a party — they played hard and lived harder — and that was a legacy that would live on in Swift Current for a long time. But now they were, in the words of Buck Owens, "together again."

If only getting together had been that easy.…

Kennedy hadn't been the least bit reluctant to join up with his old buddies again. In fact, he was looking forward to the drive and the chatter that would be involved. He just didn't know whether he wanted to go back to Swift Current, and he had spent a lot of quiet time arguing with himself: "Should I go or should I stay? Should I stay or should I go?"

"I was very hesitant about going," Kennedy admits. "But I needed to face it. Christ, I've been running away from everything my whole life. The difference is that I've dealt with that stuff.… I'm not — and I hate the word *victim* — I'm not held hostage by Graham or what happened. I feel it's part of my life. It did happen. It's not that it didn't change certain things of the way I live my life."

In time, Kennedy chose to make the trip. And, in the end, he was glad that he did.

"It was just a real good closure piece for me," he admits. "I had always had this inner fear of going back there. I don't have that anymore."

When pressed, Kennedy admits that he really didn't know whether he would find closure. After all, what he had undergone during his time in Swift Current was unspeakably horrific. Who knew what might happen upon his return for the first time in twenty years?

"The reality of what came out of there was just real good closure for everybody," Kennedy says. "It was about just being able to shoot the poop and express views that … I think people had wanted to express for a long time."

Kennedy, who is prone to speaking in the majestic "we," also admits to having felt huge relief at "actually being able to leave there and close the door and know that we never had to go back there."

Sheldon Kennedy (left) and Bob Wilkie at a Broncos' Booster Club skate.

Wilkie felt pretty much the same way. He was excited about spending some time with Kennedy and Soberlak on the drive to Swift Current, but he had his doubts about what awaited them.

"I was going to be with my buddies again," Wilkie says, "but I did not know what was going to happen. We had been through so much together but never talked about so much of it."

Earlier in 2009, Wilkie had made a business trip to Calgary and had been able to hook up with Kennedy.

"It was such a powerful meeting," Wilkie recalls. "We shared insights we had not ever talked about."

They talked about the Broncos and their pro careers and what had followed.

"Shelly and I had been together for a couple of years in Detroit's organization after we left Swift," Wilkie says. "Things had gone downhill for both of us after we left. Sheldon had gotten in trouble for drinking … as had I."

They both were known, as Wilkie puts it, "as troubled players [who] liked to party … that type of thing."

The truth, however, was something else. It wasn't that the two of them liked to party. It wasn't that they liked the taste of the copious amounts of booze they ingested.

"The truth was," Wilkie now admits, "we were numbing ourselves. We had been through things no one could comprehend, and because we were not allowed to talk about it, we dealt with it the only way we knew how: by drinking."

CHAPTER 2

The Crash

December 30, 1986.

When the day dawned in the southwestern Saskatchewan city of Swift Current, it brought with it a taste of January. It would turn into one of those wet winter storms that you have to live through to understand. Biting winds. Wet snow — or is it rain, or sleet? — blowing at you in a horizontal fashion, stinging your face like so many wasps.

But no matter how hard it tried, the storm that day couldn't do anything to dash the optimism that surrounded the Swift Current Broncos, the city's brand new and oh-so-popular Western Hockey League team. The players had just reconvened after going home for Christmas. They had returned full of hope and exuberance; they were bound and determined that the second half of this season was going to carry them into the playoffs.

While the weather, which had been so good the day before, had turned nasty, the Broncos skated that morning and the vibe was good. They were flying around the ice surface, eager for that evening's game against the host Regina Pats. The team bus was scheduled to leave at 2:30 p.m., but with a two-hour drive ahead of them and because the roads were bad, it was decided they would leave a little earlier.

But one thing led to another, and the bus didn't roll out of the Civic Centre parking lot until 3:35 p.m. A couple of minutes later, the bus, with veteran driver Dave Archibald behind the wheel, turned onto the Trans-Canada Highway and headed east.

The bus would never reach its destination. In fact, it wouldn't get too far from its home base.

As often happens in these situations, one can look back and see fate's finger. Was that an omen? And what about this other incident?

The night before the accident, a few of the Broncos — including defenceman Ed Brost, a nineteen-year-old Calgarian, and forward Tracy Egeland, a sixteen-year-old from Lethbridge — had gone to a movie. In order to make curfew, they got Egeland home first, and Brost then borrowed Egeland's car and drove himself home.

Egeland, one of the team's youngest players, looked up to Brost and trusted him enough to let him take his first sports car, a red Pontiac Fiero that his parents had bought him.

Unfortunately, the weather turned during the night. As Brost was returning the car that morning, he was broadsided by another vehicle while attempting a left turn. Brost remembers having two thoughts: "The first thing … was how bad I felt for this old guy who just hit me, because I could see how shaken up he was. Second, I kept thinking, 'What am I gonna tell Tracy?'"

Although the Fiero was badly damaged and would require extensive repairs, Brost managed to drive it to Egeland's place.

"I felt like such a schmuck," Brost recalls, "and I remember the walkway to the front door seemed like it was two miles long."

When Egeland answered Brost's knock, the words spilled off Brost's tongue: "We gotta go, but I gotta tell you something."

Egeland recalls, "He felt real bad about wrecking my car, but I wasn't mad at him. I could never be mad at Ed. He was too nice a guy."

Brost and Egeland were still able to make it to the arena in time for the morning skate, after which the players ran the arena stairs for a workout. There was a lot of chatter about how important it was to start the second half of the WHL season with a bang.

The team gathered at Thumpers, a local restaurant, for lunch, then it was back to their homes for a pre-trip rest.

As the players napped, the weather got progressively worse. Bob Wilkie, who was a defenceman on the team, recalls that "many of the players felt that maybe we should stay home."

"By then," Wilkie remembers, "there was a travel advisory in effect. But, regardless of the warning, the coaches told us we were going. So we started to load the bus and prepared to depart."

However, there was a delay.

Scott Kruger, a nineteen-year-old centre who was from Swift Current, had forgotten his dress clothes, so the entire team had to wait while he hurried home to save himself a fine. Like most teams, the Broncos had a rule that required players to wear dress clothes on road trips. Players would change into track suits on the bus and then change back into their dress clothes as the bus neared its destination.

By the time Kruger returned, it was 3:30 p.m., meaning things were behind schedule. And the weather wasn't getting any better. When the bus rolled out of the arena parking lot, it was 3:35 p.m. Despite the weather, the players were excited. This would be their first post-Christmas game and they really wanted to play well.

As the bus hit the road, the talk was about that night's game and recently received Christmas gifts. The Sony Walkman was a popular item that Christmas; many of the players had received one and were preparing to listen to their favourite music.

As winger Trent Kresse, one of the team's twenty-year-olds, boarded the bus, he stopped briefly at the front to talk with *Swift Current Sun* sports writer Brian Costello about the Christmas holiday. Once the bus left the parking lot, Kresse, who was from Kindersley, Saskatchewan, excused himself, explaining that he heard a card game calling from the back.

Five minutes later, the bus turned onto the Trans-Canada Highway and began the short — well, short for the WHL — drive to Regina.

Egeland tried to sit in the back with the veterans, but a pre-Christmas episode involving vomiting and a jacket meant the veterans, led by Wilkie, put the run on the fresh-faced rookie. Egeland ended up closer to the front of the bus, seated with Brost, who was being razzed about his misfortune with Egeland's car.

Wilkie was seated in the last row of the bus, taking up the four seats on the driver's side. On the other side, directly across the aisle from him, were Kresse, Kruger, and two others. One was Chris Mantyka, a hard-nosed nineteen-year-old from Saskatoon who was known affectionately by his teammates as "Chief," and the other was Brent Ruff, a sixteen-year-old from Warburg, Alberta, who was a member of hockey's Ruff family.

As they did on virtually all trips, the four got out a deck of cards and started a game of Kaiser, a four-player game that involves partners.

And then it happened.

"You know how when you cross from one side of the road to the other, there's that little hump?" Wilkie asks. "If you close your eyes, you feel like your insides have lifted, if only for a second or two. I felt the bus moving like we were changing lanes."

The RCMP later determined that the bus was travelling at thirty-three miles per hour — fifty-three kilometres per hour — when it began its long skid.

Wilkie was plugged into his new Walkman and was reading *The Long Walk*, a book by Stephen King. To this day, Wilkie remembers that the book's cover "features an eerie picture of a windy road and a skeleton off to the side." He also remembers that he was listening to the Canadian rock group Trooper. "I had the volume turned up — the track, which I remember like it was yesterday, was 'We're Here for a Good Time (Not a Long Time)' — but not loud enough to drown out the noise of the bus."

Kresse was the first person to say anything.

"Hold on," he yelled. "It'll be okay."

And then the noise started....

"I had no idea we were going off the road. But we did," Wilkie says. "The bus left the road, rolled onto one side, bounced back to its wheels, hit the approach road, flew into the air, came crashing down on its rear tires, tipped, and skidded to a stop on its right side."

More than anything, Wilkie remembers people and things — suitcases, pillows — flying through the space inside the bus. He hit his head on the luggage rack and momentarily lost consciousness.

It was, he said, "like a war movie. Everyone was screaming, everything was everywhere. Jackets, luggage, seats, glass ... everything was all over the place."

Peter Soberlak had been seated near Wilkie. "Wilks ... Wilks ... you okay?" Soberlak called.

Wilkie had a sharp pain in his right hip and a numbness in his head.

"I think so," Wilkie answered. "But my hip really hurts and my ears won't stop ringing. Are you okay?"

"This is bad, Wilks," Soberlak replied, as he began to survey the carnage.

Soberlak had been seated against a right-side window, right in front of the four card players. Clarke Polglase, a seventeen-year-old Edmontonian, was sitting with him. They had been talking about how enjoyable the Christmas break had been. Soberlak was in mid-sentence when he realized something was wrong.

He would end up with a severely bruised right arm, the result of the bus's right side twice being hammered against the ground. To this day, he has no idea how he survived while four teammates who were seated in such close proximity didn't make it.

"Sore. I wasn't injured; just sore," Soberlak says. "I couldn't even get out of bed the next morning. I wasn't injured and this far behind my head" — he holds his hands a foot apart — "four guys are dead. So I wasn't really injured at all."

Soberlak helped Wilkie get to his feet. When they looked around, what they saw was total chaos.

The bus was on its right side. People were screaming. Debris was everywhere.

Soberlak took a look at Wilkie and said, "Your face is bleeding pretty bad. You sure you're okay?"

A bitterly cold wind was howling through what had been the rear window. Wilkie, who always wore shorts and flip-flops on the bus, suddenly was cold. He wanted his coat and shoes. So he reached down and started to pull up the seats that were lying on the ground. What he saw would haunt him forever.

"There was a pair of legs there but nothing else," he says. "The rest of the body obviously was under the bus."

Wilkie dropped the seat and started to scream, "Get off the bus! Get off the friggin' bus! Someone is underneath the bus!"

Soberlak and Wilkie then heard a noise from behind them. When they turned, they saw Mantyka. He was under the bus, lying on his back, and the bus was crushing him. Mantyka was still alive; he was gasping for air and had blood trickling from one side of his mouth.

Soberlak and Wilkie held each other in an attempt to gain control of their shaking. They continued to yell for everyone to get off the bus.

"Chief [Mantyka] was reaching out for help, but there was nothing we could do," Wilkie says. "Never in my life had I ever felt so helpless or scared. We just kept screaming and screaming and screaming, and when we looked back again, Chief was gone."

Soberlak remembers Kurt Lackten, the nineteen-year-old team captain, helping players get out of the debris-filled bus.

"He was probably the last one to leave. They were getting all of us out of there," Soberlak says, adding that because he and Wilkie had been seated in the back of the bus, they knew what most of their teammates didn't.

"We had to go out the front," Soberlak explains. "In that time, when everyone was moving up to the front, that's when me and Bob watched Chris. We knew how serious it was but nobody else did. Nobody up front really knew what had happened or what had gone on."

Before moving to the front and exiting, Soberlak and Wilkie looked through the gaping rear window and noticed people gathered around what looked to be two more bodies.

Wilkie's system, however, couldn't take it. His face was a bloody mess. He had just watched one teammate die. Now there appeared to be two more bodies near the bus.

He was stressed, cold, and in pain and shock.

He blacked out.

Leesa Culp wasn't yet married in 1986, and was returning to Moose Jaw after spending Christmas with her family — the Krafts — in Penticton, British Columbia. A student at a bible college in Moose Jaw, she had caught a ride with a trucker and, as fate would have it, was right behind the Broncos' bus.

The trucker had slowed down in order to allow the bus onto the Trans-Canada Highway as it left Swift Current.

Culp witnessed the crash and, in fact, left the truck to survey the damage and see if she could be of any help.

"As I walked quickly toward the back of the bus," Culp recalls, "I noticed a body maybe fifteen to twenty feet to the right of the rear of the bus, face down in the field of snow."

It was Scott Kruger.

"To the left of that body, a little closer to the bus, was another body lying on its back. His one leg pointed toward the open field, and his other leg was all twisted up — bent badly at the knee. His head was pointed toward the bus. His eyes were open wide and glassy looking. I walked around to the left side of his body and knelt down to take his left hand, thinking I might be able to get a pulse."

It was Trent Kresse.

"Seconds later, other people were gathering around both bodies in the field, trying to revive them. I stood up and backed out of the way and was looking around. It was then that I saw someone's head sticking out from under the bus. Beside that head there was a pair of legs sticking out from the bus. It was obvious that they were the head and legs of two different people because of the distance between them."

They were Chris Mantyka and Brent Ruff.

Lonnie Spink, a nineteen-year-old right winger from Sherwood Park, Alberta, who had been acquired from the Kamloops Blazers in November, had been seated near the front of the bus. Defenceman Gord Green, also nineteen, from Medley, Alberta, was beside him, and Ian Herbers, another nineteen-year-old defenceman, was across the aisle. Spink, Green, and Herbers, who was from Jasper, Alberta, knew each other from playing together in Sherwood Park.

Spink remembers hearing someone yell, "Hold on!"

After that, he says, it was like everything was happening in slow motion. But it wasn't until after it was all over that he realized the bus had actually become airborne and had ended up on its right side.

"It was like a shotgun had blown out the windows," Spink says.

As the bus flew through the air and landed hard, Herbers was thrown across the aisle. Somehow, he ended up in the luggage rack. Once he extricated himself, he and Spink frantically searched for Green. It turned out that they actually were walking on him — a dazed Green had ended up buried under some luggage.

Spink and Herbers uncovered Green and they all hugged each other. Bruised and bleeding from facial cuts, they were happy to have survived

Gord Green (right) during one of his deployments, this one in the summer of 2006.

but blissfully unaware of what had happened in the rear of the bus.

Then they heard someone from the back of the bus yelling for everyone to get out because players were trapped underneath it. They quickly exited and were met by passersby who had stopped and were now getting the players into vehicles and whisking them to the hospital. Once at the hospital, they all phoned their families.

Spink remembers telling his family that he was okay and that no one he knew was hurt. At that point, he still didn't know who was hurt, or that anyone had been killed. And having been in Swift Current for only three weeks, he didn't know Kresse, Kruger, Mantyka, or Ruff very well.

It wasn't until later that night that Spink learned he had lost four teammates in an accident from which he had escaped virtually unscathed.

The next day, Spink and Herbers visited bus driver Dave Archibald. They wanted Archibald to know that this tragedy was an accident, that it was just bad luck, that it wasn't his fault.

"We sat down with Dave and his wife over sandwiches and told him we still trusted him with our lives," Spink says. "I will always remember the utter look of sadness on Dave's face. I wish him the best.

"It was a day that changed all of our lives forever."

Green, a rugged defenceman, would go on to spend twenty years in the Canadian military. A combat engineer, he would serve in Kuwait, Croatia, Bosnia, Kosovo, and Afghanistan.

Through all of that, he said, he never forgot his time in Swift Current.

Green had spent the previous season with the Lethbridge Broncos. The franchise was sold and relocated to Swift Current for the 1986–87 season, and Green moved with it.

"The biggest thing for me about Swift Current was the fans," Green said. "I played in Lethbridge the season before, and to move to Swift was not something that the players looked forward to the summer before the first season. A lot of the veteran players asked to be traded without even going to Swift.

"That all changed the first time we went to Swift Current. The fans treated us great right from day one. After the crash, they took us in like family. I still have a special place in my heart for the city and the people."

CHAPTER 3

The Broncos Come Home

Swift Current is a community of more than sixteen thousand people, located on the Trans-Canada Highway in the southwestern corner of Saskatchewan. The city gets its name from a creek that meanders across the prairie, eventually emptying into the South Saskatchewan River. The Cree who camped alongside the creek for centuries referred to it as *kisiskaciwan*, which means "it flows swiftly." Fur traders later named it *Rivière au Courant*, meaning "river that runs," hence Swift Current (a.k.a. Speedy Creek).

Best known as a farming community, Swift Current is typical of many small towns and cities across North America. Everyone knows everyone. Friends went to school together, and now their children go to those same schools together. It is a tightly knit community in which everyone supports each other, especially in times of need. When everything is running smoothly, there is the usual gossip and chatter about the neighbours. There is some crime, and there are a few skeletons. Oh, and there is a Walmart and a casino.

For the most part, Swift Current, like many places its size, is a stable and supportive community.

What is not typical, though, is the life-altering tragedy that occurred on December 30, 1986.

The welcoming sign outside Swift Current. It reads, "Where Life Makes Sense."

Despite the town slogan — "Swift Current: Where Life Makes Sense," which is engraved on a granite slab on the city's outskirts — nothing about what happened on that day made sense.

When the bus accident happened, the Broncos were in their first season in Swift Current, having relocated from Lethbridge after the 1985–86 season.

The Broncos would rebound from the tragic accident to make the playoffs in the spring of 1987. And two years later they would win the Memorial Cup. This truly is one of the great stories in the history of Canadian sports.

But when you throw in what would come after that — with Sheldon Kennedy, one of the team's stars, accusing Graham James, the team's general manager and head coach, of sexually assaulting him more than three hundred times — it becomes a horribly tragic story. It is a story that, when looked at in whole, has more twists and turns than the most imaginative writer could concoct. Even the backroom dealing that resulted in the Broncos returning to Swift Current is a story in itself.

Swift Current hadn't had a WHL team to call its own since the spring of 1974, when it lost its franchise to Lethbridge. Now, twelve years later, the Broncos had come home.

The Broncos weren't a chartered member of the Canadian Major Junior Hockey League, later the WHL, when it was born in the summer of 1966. But they came on board for the second season, 1967–68, as the CMJHL morphed into the Western Canada Junior Hockey League. The Broncos would play out of Swift Current through the end of the 1973–74 season. After that season, owner Bill Burton relocated the franchise to Lethbridge.

Now it was 1986, and the Broncos were back in the 2,235-seat Centennial Civic Centre. A group of enthusiastic business people and civic politicians, led by John Rittinger, a local engineer who had long pursued a WHL franchise for his beloved city, had purchased the Lethbridge Broncos from Dennis Kjelgaard.

In the early 1980s, Rittinger was president of the junior A Broncos, who played in the Saskatchewan Junior Hockey League, but that level of hockey just wasn't selling. So, even though he didn't have a franchise, Rittinger began selling shares and season tickets for a major junior team.

(Think about that for a moment and you realize that it's the same approach taken by Jim Balsillie, the co-CEO of Research in Motion, when he felt in 2008 that he was close to purchasing the NHL's Nashville Predators and relocating the franchise to southern Ontario.)

"If I knew then what I know now," Rittinger told the *Regina Leader-Post* during the 1989 Memorial Cup tournament in Saskatoon, "we would have had a franchise then. I wanted it all paid for."

Rittinger said his group had $200,000 and had sold seven hundred season tickets in 1982, but he "decided it wasn't enough to go ahead, so I gave it all back." Later, Rittinger would form an alliance with Pat Ginnell, a veteran of western Canada's hockey wars, who was operating the Swift Current Indians, playing in the junior A Saskatchewan Junior Hockey League. According to Rittinger, they ended up selling 150 shares, "most of them at $2,000." A ten-man board, with Rittinger as president, was elected at a shareholders' meeting.

Rittinger would go on to lead attempts to purchase and relocate numerous franchises, among them the Kelowna Wings, Calgary

Wranglers, Kamloops Junior Oilers, Regina Pats, New Westminster Bruins, Seattle Breakers....

He came oh so close to purchasing the Regina Pats during the first half of the 1985–86 season. So close, in fact, that the Pats actually postponed a home game in preparation for a midseason move to Swift Current. But it was a sale — by Saskatoon's Pinder family — that never went through.

Remarkably, the genesis of this situation was a $1 parking fee that was about to be implemented by Regina Exhibition Park, which controlled the Agridome, as the home of the Pats then was known. The Pats' owners and fans were in a lather over the approach of paid parking, even at $1, and it almost cost them their franchise.

"I was building a new home and fell down some stairs and hurt my back," Rittinger said. "I was in hospital and had a phone in my room. Herb [Pinder Jr.] called and asked if I wanted to buy the team. So we worked on that."

In fact, two games originally scheduled for Regina were rescheduled for Swift Current just after Christmas.

"Can you imagine all those banners in the [Swift Current Centennial] Civic Centre?" Rittinger said, referring to the many championship banners the Pats have won and which hang in their home arena. "It was preposterous, but it looked like it was going to happen. Then the league bought the team and sold it" to a group that included former NHLer Bill Hicke.

Had the Pats/Swift Current deal gone through, Rittinger said, "Herb would have operated the team in Swift Current for the rest of the season. We would have just come to games and watched."

And then there were the attempts to purchase all those other franchises....

With Kelowna, Rittinger said, they did a lot of talking, but "we never did get a signed agreement."

Which wasn't the case when it came to the Wranglers. "We had a signed agreement with the Wranglers. Then Brian Ekstrom came along and bought them."

Late in 1984, the Swift Current group also had a signed agreement with Seattle owner John Hamilton.

"He ended up in Swift Current one night," Rittinger recalled. "It got to the point where we controlled the [player] list. We sent Kevin Ginnell, one of Paddy's sons, to Seattle to manage the list. The WHL had to approve the sale. It refused." The WHL, not wanting a West Coast team to move east, bought the franchise.

That wasn't the first time the Breakers were almost sold. On June 15, 1983, the *Lethbridge Herald* reported, "The owner of the Seattle Breakers said he has reached an agreement to sell the WHL team. Terms of the sale by Breakers' owner John Hamilton to Dennis Kjelgaard, former owner of the WHL's Lethbridge Broncos, have not been disclosed. Hamilton, who has sought a buyer, said Kjelgaard 'is just waiting to see something in writing.'"

Kjelgaard had purchased the Lethbridge Broncos from Bill Burton and later sold the franchise. Now, it seems, he was trying to get back in. As it turned out, he wouldn't buy the Breakers. Instead, he bought the Broncos again. All told, Kjelgaard was involved with the Broncos for eleven of their twelve seasons in Lethbridge, but cited sagging attendance — the Broncos averaged 1,600 fans in 1985–86 and drew only 647 fans to their final playoff game — and burgeoning expenses as reasons for his decision to get out.

In the meantime, Rittinger said, "We were buying Kamloops from the Edmonton Oilers. A Kamloops group owned around thirty percent and had first right of refusal. They had to come up with the money by a certain day and got it on the last day. They were selling T-shirts that read, 'Where the Hell Is Swift Current?'"

Rittinger, who was telling his story after the Broncos had won the 1989 Memorial Cup, added, "I wonder if they know now?"

And then there were the Winnipeg Warriors.

"Winnipeg was supposed to transfer to Moose Jaw," Rittinger said, adding that it almost didn't happen after he and Art DeFehr of the Winnipeg ownership group "shook hands at a meeting in Calgary. We went to [WHL president] Ed Chynoweth and said we had bought the team. Moose Jaw had defaulted several times."

In fact, according to Rittinger, Moose Jaw was to have presented a $10,000 cheque for the bond. However, DeFehr checked with "the bank and the bank said the money wasn't there."

The league gave Moose Jaw "a couple more days and they came up with the money. So we lost that one."

By then, Paddy Ginnell was coaching the New Westminster Bruins, who were owned by Ron Dixon, an old-school operator if ever there was one. If the price was right, he would sell.

"Paddy says we can get this franchise," Rittinger related. "Dixon calls one day at 3:00 a.m. He says, 'Give me $300,000 and we'll leave the team in New Westminster and we'll run it but you'll own it.'" Rittinger may have been born at night, but it hadn't been that night.

There also was an attempt to buy the Brandon Wheat Kings.

"Mrs. [Anne] Ross called and said, 'I own x per cent of this club. I think I can buy up some and own fifty percent. Then you can buy it and move it.' Paddy went to Brandon and said, 'We'll buy your team for $270,000.' The league would never go for that.

"Oh, and I spoke to Fraser McColl [who owned the Victoria Cougars], but didn't get too far with that," Rittinger said.

The WHL, Rittinger had come to believe, wasn't the least bit interested in returning to Swift Current.

But, before he could get too discouraged, Rittinger began hearing whispers about Kjelgaard and Al Foder perhaps wanting to sell the Lethbridge Broncos, the franchise that had originated in Swift Current. The Broncos had won one WHL championship (1982–83) in twelve seasons in the southern Alberta city.

"Kjelgaard calls Paddy and says, 'I'll sell you half a franchise; we'll have a draft and divide up the players and have two teams, one in Lethbridge and one in Swift Current,'" Rittinger said.

By now, Rittinger said, the Swift Current group and Ginnell had had something of a falling out. But the group's nest egg had grown to more than $300,000.

"Denny comes down to Swift Current," Rittinger recalled. "He says $500,000. It was a ten-minute meeting and he went back to Lethbridge."

As talks continued, Ed Chynoweth became involved as an arbitrator of sorts and helped settle it.

"I think Ed got tired of us," Rittinger said with a chuckle.

In the end, Rittinger's bunch paid between $400,000 and $450,000 for its WHL team. (The Edmonton Oil Kings, the last expansion franchise sold by the WHL, cost the NHL's Edmonton Oilers a cool $4 million. The Oil Kings began play in the 2007–08 season. The Kamloops Blazers, a more established franchise, sold for more than $6 million in the fall of 2007.)

Some of the teams that Rittinger had tried to purchase didn't stay put for long. The Kelowna Wings became the Spokane Chiefs for the 1985–86 season. The Calgary Wranglers, who had moved west from Winnipeg for the 1977–78 season, ended up in Lethbridge as the Hurricanes in time for 1987–88. The New Westminster Bruins became the Tri-City Americans over the summer of 1988.

In 1988–89, a season in which the Broncos would win the Memorial Cup, there were fourteen teams in the WHL. At one time or another, Rittinger had tried to buy eleven of them. Only the Medicine Hat Tigers, Prince Albert Raiders, and Saskatoon Blades hadn't heard from him.

But now a sale had gone through; the WHL's board of governors gave its unanimous approval on April 11, 1986, just three days after the Broncos' last season in Lethbridge had come to an end. Rittinger's perseverance and diligence had paid off — Swift Current Tier One Franchise Inc., headed by Rittinger, owned the Broncos. The WHL was back in Swift Current.

Buying the franchise was one thing, of course. It took an untold amount of work to take the franchise from there to the ice, and there was the matter of a budget approaching $600,000, a large sum for a franchise operating in the Canadian Hockey League's smallest market.

But it all got done in time for the 1986–87 season.

CHAPTER 4

The RCMP Officer

On December 30, 1986, at 3:45 p.m., a call for emergency assistance was heard on the scanner in the RCMP detachment at Swift Current. A bus had overturned east of town on the Trans-Canada Highway.

Corporal Bob Harriman, an RCMP officer since 1974, was on duty when the call came in. Immediately upon being contacted by the radio dispatch centre, Harriman knew he was responding to a situation in which there were likely to be multiple injuries and perhaps fatalities. En route to the accident site, he was further advised by the dispatcher that there were at least four dead and an unknown number of injured.

The heavy slush and ice covering the roads was a challenge, even for a seasoned law enforcement officer like Harriman. However, with his hands tightly gripping the steering wheel of his vehicle, Harriman wasn't just worried about the road conditions.

After all, it wasn't a commercial passenger bus that had crashed: it was the bus carrying Swift Current's beloved junior hockey team. When Harriman heard that, his mind reeled, and he had to pause and regroup. The fact that the Broncos were involved made it personal — really personal. Harriman and his family — wife Janine and daughters Suzie and Cari — provided room and board for defenceman Bob Wilkie. He had been billeted in their home since the Broncos acquired him from the Calgary Wranglers. Like most billet families, the Harrimans had gotten close to the seventeen-year-old Wilkie over the previous three months, and by now he was all but part of the family.

Billet families provide a home away from home for junior hockey players, and the relationships that are forged are often unbreakable. Any billet mom will tell you that "her" hockey player is like a son to her. It is not unusual for a billet family to be there when their player gets married or debuts in his first NHL game. It also isn't unusual for a real, true friendship to grow between a player's billet family and his parents.

Despite Harriman's personal connection to the accident, however, he was first and foremost a professional; he knew he had a job to do, and he set out to do it.

Upon his arrival at the scene of the crash, Harriman noticed the presence of other police units and saw that plastic yellow sheets had been placed over four bodies. Police officers and emergency medical services personnel were, according to Harriman, "triaging injured for transportation via ambulance or available vehicles" that had happened upon the scene.

The Broncos' bus had ended up on its right side, and the space that at one time had contained the front windshield had been used as an emergency exit. Harriman observed that twelve to fifteen people with various injuries were gathered in the highway's south ditch.

"Many were capable of walking and had moved from the bus to the side of the roadway," he recalls. "Others had exited the bus but remained on the ground in the ditch."

At the time of the call, Harriman had been driving a police van, so he was able to transport six of the injured, including general manager and head coach Graham James, to the hospital in Swift Current. The hospital was about a ten-minute drive from the accident scene.

"James appeared to be in shock," Harriman recalls, "and was crying and saying 'Why?' over and over."

(More than twenty years later, Harriman would look back at everything and offer this: "A twist of pitiful irony also unfolded that day, as I transported Graham James and a couple of injured players to the Swift Current Hospital. I recall his grief toward his players, which was to be overshadowed by investigations into his sexual misconduct involving his players.")

After turning over the injured to hospital staff, Harriman, almost sick with worry over the fate of Wilkie, returned to the accident scene. In the short time that he had been on site and during his first trip to the hospital and back, he "hadn't accounted for Bob as either a survivor or one of the injured."

Mind racing and heart pounding, Harriman entered the bus through what used to be the windshield. Scrambling over what had been the right-hand seats, he searched for injured, trapped, or dead passengers. Harriman felt a brief sense of relief when he realized "the bus was clear of survivors." That left only the four bodies to be checked, something Harriman didn't want to think about, not even for one second.

During an RCMP career that began in Humboldt, Saskatchewan, in 1974 and ended in the Lower Mainland of British Columbia in 2010, Harriman attended hundreds of fatal accidents.

"But," he admits, "this one in particular remains the most vivid and difficult scene I have witnessed."

In Swift Current, Harriman was working as a forensic identification specialist, so one of his responsibilities was to capture the accident scene on film and gather evidence, which he did as he moved through and around the site.

Lifting each of the plastic yellow sheets and looking into the faces of the young men who had been enjoying a card game just a short time before would be difficult enough, but not knowing whether he would lift a blanket and find Wilkie's dead eyes staring back at him made things that much worse.

Harriman prepared to check under each of the yellow covers. By now he felt physically ill. His forehead was wet, but he didn't know if it was sweat from nervous anxiety or from snow melting as it landed on his face. With great trepidation, he lifted the cover off one of the victims who had been pinned under the bus. It wasn't Wilkie. But there are no words to express his mixed emotions in the moment.

Harriman moved further outside toward the other three blankets.

"I uncovered each boy, recognizing some, and fearing the next one would be Bob," Harriman says.

Upon completing the ghastly task, Harriman was torn — he was relieved to realize that Wilkie wasn't one of the four players who had been killed, but he felt tremendous sorrow because four boys were dead.

For their families, for the survivors and their families, and for the citizens of Swift Current, life would never be the same, and Harriman knew it.

Most of the other players, coaches, and team officials, as well as the driver, Doug Archibald, were injured to one degree or another. The physical injuries would heal; the mental hurt would linger for a long, long time.

"I don't think you ever get over it," Peter Soberlak, one of the Broncos, would say more than twenty years later. "It's a cliché, but you never get over something like that because it drastically changes your perspective on life.

"It made my hockey seem really not all that important at that point."

While thoughts of the impact the accident would have on the team and the community raced through Harriman's mind, he continued to be faced with one pressing question: What had happened to Bob Wilkie?

The Harrimans had gotten involved as billets out of their sheer love for hockey. Bob was a career RCMP officer — he had even been part of the famed Musical Ride in 1977 and 1978 — and Janine was employed by Scotiabank. Janine's four brothers, like so many young Canadian males, had played hockey, and she had grown up watching *Hockey Night in Canada*. With the Broncos franchise returning to Swift Current from Lethbridge, the Harrimans jumped at the chance to be a part of what most of the community felt was a homecoming.

When Bob Wilkie came to live with the Harrimans, they had two small children, Suzie and Cari, and another on the way. On May 8, 1987, five months after the bus accident, they welcomed a baby boy into their family. They chose to name him Patrick, after Broncos goaltender Pat Nogier, who was Wilkie's good friend. Nogier would often visit Wilkie at the Harriman home, and they found him to be extremely likeable.

Janine remembers, "We had Bob as a billet for a total of three years. He became one of the family, especially through all the challenges and difficulties endured by the players during the Graham James era, beginning with the bus accident and ending with the coaching scandal."

Bob Wilkie, with former billets Janine and Bob Harriman (2008).

After the Broncos won the 1989 Memorial Cup and had returned to Swift Current from Saskatoon, the site of the tournament, the Harrimans held a barbecue as a prelude to the partying. The Harriman children and others from around the neighbourhood watched as the Broncos barbecued wieners with the plastic on them. (Hey, these were hockey players, not culinary arts students.) During the barbecue, Wilkie began spinning the youngest Harriman daughter, Suzie, above his head. After he put her down, she staggered around like a catcher under a wind-blown popup, only to receive a gash when she fell and hit her head on the fireplace. Which is how Suzie got her Memorial Cup souvenir.

Janine fondly remembers long talks around the kitchen table, and becoming a surrogate parent to a young man who affected her family in more ways than they ever could have imagined.

Of the accident, Bob Harriman says, "It was a memorable but tragic moment: looking under body blankets for my hockey son, but also looking for that young boy who arrived at our home full of dreams to be the next superstar in hockey, who was bewildered and so very unprepared for his new environment, who was confused by the mixed messages of agents and coaches, and so very young to be thrust on his new billet family at sixteen years old. What I saw in each young face that day was something that no one can imagine. The dead would speak no more and the injured would carry scars forever."

Because of his job, Harriman spent a lot of time involved with the accident and its aftermath.

"The days and weeks after the accident I spent working on the accident scene by day and dealing with Bob's injuries and post-traumatic syndrome by night," Harriman remembers. "Bob had ongoing visions of witnessing three of his friends fall into the open window area of the bus and disappear under the bus as it moved along the ditch. His most difficult time was dealing with the friend who, when the bus came to rest, was still alive but pinned under and slightly inside the bus.

"Janine spent hours at the hospital with Bob. We would spend many hours helping Bob cope with his conflicted emotions as he had been sitting in the bus seats most impacted by the crash. He had witnessed the dying moments of the young boys who had become his friends, and suffered both the fear of the crash and the scene repeating itself over and over in his mind.

"Bob also suffered the 'survivor syndrome,' and often said, 'If I could have only done something to help one of them or save any of them....'"

All Harriman could do was tell Wilkie over and over again that neither he nor anyone else could have saved anyone that day.

CHAPTER 5

The Hospital

Bob Wilkie awoke in Swift Current Union Hospital. As his eyes opened, all of his senses began to take in all that was going on around him.

"When I came to," he says, "I remembered immediately what had happened, and I couldn't shake the image I had in my head of Chris Mantyka."

Needless to say, the hospital was a beehive of activity. But at the same time, a pall seemed to hang over the building. People were scurrying every which way and there were unanswered questions hanging out in every corner. This was a small hospital that served Swift Current and surrounding area, and bus accidents that included fatalities weren't a run-of-the-mill occurrence.

By now, word of the accident had gotten out into the community, and family members and billets, hopeful and fearing the worst at the same time, had begun congregating at the hospital. Everyone was looking for news — any tidbit of news.

Wilkie had asked someone at the hospital to call Janine Harriman, who hurried to be at his side. He had a hip injury — he was fearful that it had been broken — but hadn't yet been taken for X-rays. Upon her arrival, Janine, four months pregnant with Patrick, quickly realized that Wilkie was going to be fine. But she found the hospital a sombre place, with several players wandering aimlessly around the emergency ward, clearly overcome with grief and shock, clearly dazed and confused.

Janine was shown to Wilkie's room, where the two had an emotional reunion. As best he could, Wilkie related what had happened. She held one of his hands and wept as emotion poured out of him.

In times of stress, people sometimes say the strangest things, and this was no exception.

"Janine," Wilkie said, "all I have on is my Christmas boxers. Can you get me some shorts or something?"

He remembers something resembling painful laughter coming from Janine.

"It was total chaos and all I could think about was my underwear," Wilkie says. "We held each other and cried some more."

Wilkie asked Janine to call his parents with the news that he was okay. That wouldn't be a problem, she said, adding that her two girls already had been told that their "big brother" would be fine.

Meanwhile, Janine's husband, Corporal Bob Harriman, would spend several hours doing investigative work at the accident site before being able to get back to the hospital, where he found his wife and Wilkie comforting each other.

"Picture a tough hockey player sitting on a hospital bed close to his billet mom in Santa Claus boxers," he says.

While the Harrimans and Wilkie held a teary reunion, players were continually being wheeled past the room. On their way by, players would glance into the room, recognize Wilkie, and ask if he was okay. Some of them asked if he had seen Scott Kruger, Trent Kresse, Chris Mantyka, or Brent Ruff.

After a while, Wilkie was able to compose himself enough to tell Janine that he had seen Mantyka die and that "there had been at least one other player trapped under the bus."

It was about then when Graham James, the team's general manager and head coach, happened by. He darted into Wilkie's room and asked if they had seen Joe Sakic and Sheldon Kennedy.

"That was it," Wilkie says. "He didn't ask, 'Are you okay?' He didn't ask, 'Did you hear about Scotty and Trent?' He didn't ask, 'Did you hear about Brent and Chris?' All he said was, 'Have you seen Joe and Sheldon?'"

Bob Wilkie with his father, Jim, mother, Judy, and brother, Scott.

Courtesy of Bob Wilkie.

Wilkie was stunned by what he interpreted as James's callousness. In hindsight, he says that it was then, in that hospital room, when he began to look at James in a completely different light.

"It didn't make any sense to me," Wilkie says, adding that he was left wondering, *What about me? I was part of his team, too.*

He admits that he turned his head away from James and "continued to cry ... and cry ... and cry."

Eventually, Wilkie was examined by a doctor. His face was scraped and covered in dried blood, but he didn't need stitches. He was taken for X-rays on his sore hip, but they came back negative. Nothing was broken.

In the meantime, things continued to happen.

Peter Soberlak remembers arriving at the hospital in a van, walking in, and realizing that a wave of urgency had overtaken the facility. It was, he felt, organized confusion.

"It was all us kids walking around ... I think there was a sense of shock with the people in the hospital, the nurses and the doctors," he says. "I remember standing there, just waiting to get behind a counter and phone my parents. That's the first thing I did, was get back there and call my folks and say that I was all right. At that point, I still didn't know what had happened. I didn't know for a while."

He had ridden from the scene of the crash to the hospital in a van with Trevor Kruger, who kept asking Soberlak if he had seen his brother, Scott. Trevor, who had been seated near the middle of the bus, knew that Soberlak had been in a seat right in front of where Scott, along with Kresse, Mantyka, and Ruff, had been playing cards.

"He knew I was in the back and he was worried about Scott," Soberlak says.

Trevor was the Broncos' rookie goaltender that season, and he would stay through the Memorial Cup–winning season of 1988–89. Being from Swift Current, he would become something of a hometown hero.

"I must admit," Wilkie says, "the first time I saw Trev play I thought, 'Who the hell is this? Why is he here?' Little did I know that he was to be one of the main reasons we won the Memorial Cup. He played the puck like a defenceman and was very quick and agile."

Trevor was not yet four months past his eighteenth birthday at the time of the crash. He called his mother, Louise, from the hospital.

"Mom," he said, "you have to come to the hospital. Something happened to Scott."

Louise and her husband, Walt, immediately headed for the hospital, where they took seats in the waiting room. Shortly after arriving, Louise found herself comforting Kari Kesslar, who was waiting for news on Trent Kresse, her fiancé.

(Later it would be revealed that Brian Costello, the *Swift Current Sun* sports writer who had spoken with Kresse on the bus, had stumbled on a set of keys in the field near the wreckage. The key fob had the name *Kari* on it. Knowing that the keys belonged to Kresse, Costello didn't have the heart to pass along something so trifling as car keys to Kari at that particular time. So he gave the keys to a member of the coaching staff, who later gave them to her.)

A few minutes after the Krugers arrived at the hospital, assistant coach Lorne Frey, who was Louise's brother, entered the waiting room and immediately told them that four players — including their son Scott — were dead.

When Wilkie and Soberlak first arrived at the hospital, they knew only that Mantyka had been killed. They knew that only because they had watched helplessly as their teammate had died, the weight of the bus crushing the life out of him.

"I'm not sure who eventually told me about the other three," Wilkie says. "At the hospital, I continued to fade in and out of consciousness, and to this day I am unable to recall who told me."

Later that night, Wilkie was moved into a room with Kurt Lackten, a forward from Kamsack, Saskatchewan, who was the Broncos' captain. According to Wilkie, they lay in their beds and talked … and talked … and talked.

"We talked about what had happened — what we knew, who had survived, and who hadn't," Wilkie remembers. "It was all very, very sad, and the weight of it was oftentimes more than we could bear. There were tears and more tears."

Lackten had been one of the last players to leave the accident site for the hospital. He had spent a lot of time trying to help people in and around the crashed bus. He emerged from the accident with cuts and bruises, as did everyone else, and was later found to have some cracked ribs.

"Kurt truly had shown a strong compassionate side to his personality by forgetting about himself and his injuries," Wilkie says. "In my eyes, he had done what heroes do."

Lackten, now a Honolulu-based commercial pilot with Hawaiian Airlines, doesn't see himself as a hero. He was the team captain — "I think it was a team vote," he says. Asked if he was always seen as a leader, Lackten pauses before saying, "I guess everybody likes to think so."

For his part, he says he has no recollection of helping people get off the bus or providing aid to them once they were outside. Over the years, he has tried to remember, he says, but there just isn't anything there.

"I really can't say," he says, when asked about his role post-accident. "I really don't remember helping people out."

He knows that, like everyone else, he exited the bus through what used to be the windshield. After that, well, "I don't really remember a whole bunch."

Lackten assumes that he can't remember because of shock, but admits that he has nothing other than personal experience on which to base that. However, he does remember his injuries, especially a four-inch gash on the back of his head. It was that gash, more than anything else, that led to his bloodied appearance.

"I remember the doctor was an old-time doctor," Lackten says with a chuckle. "I can't remember his name. He was an old-timer. I remember it being really busy and crazy there.

"I'd had tons of stitches before. Even after a game or during a game, they kind of take their time. This guy didn't take his time. He just did it as quick as he could and he moved on. I remember that. I remember thinking, *That was kind of weird.*"

It could be that Lackten remembers that episode because it left him with a souvenir of the accident.

"I don't have much hair any more and I cut it real close," he explains. "You can see that scar — it's a real butcher job. It's like he folded it over. But that's all right. It's no big deal."

He knows that he also was left with a couple of cracked ribs, but has no recollection of being taken for X-rays. He knows that when he got to the hospital, "a couple of guys were helping me and right by the door I collapsed. I think that is when I started feeling things."

He can't recall any conversations he may have had with Wilkie, but does remember Colleen and Karen MacBean visiting him in hospital. Colleen was a long-time volunteer and education consultant with the Broncos, and also billeted players in the home she shared with her husband Frank, who was on the team's board of directors. Karen, their daughter, was dating Lackten at the time.

"After that, I don't know," Lackten says. "I can't remember too much."

When Lackten finally dozed off, Wilkie found that sleep wasn't going to come easily. As he lay in bed, Wilkie found himself thinking over and over again: *Why did I survive?*

When the bus had begun its journey, he had been less than four feet from four teammates who now were dead. And now the questions — almost all of them prefaced by the word *why* — came in a torrent. It was like he had turned on a faucet and now couldn't turn it off.

"Why was I still here?"

"Why did God do this?"

"Why them?"

As Wilkie searched for sleep, he remembered his dead teammates:

"Brent, who was so young and talented and seemed to have such a bright future. Chris, with his huge smile and heart to match, who was like our big brother, always there to protect and support us. Scotty and Trent. They really were this team's leaders. They were always upbeat and extremely talented. The two of them had such a great rapport with each other that it was like a comedy act when they got going on each other. Scotty was a joker and was always stirring something up. Trent was a little quieter. But both were quick and their comebacks always made you smile."

Wilkie had hit it off with Kruger and Kresse, who were talented local boys. Kruger had played the previous season with the Prince Albert Raiders, putting up 106 points, including eighty assists, in seventy-two games. Kresse was also a point machine; he had won the Saskatchewan junior league's 1984–85 scoring championship, putting up 148 points, including 111 assists, in sixty-four games with the Swift Current franchise.

Wilkie remembers returning to the Broncos after Christmas just days before the accident and sitting down with Kresse and Kruger.

"The three of us had conversations in which we swore that we would drive each other toward our goals of being selected in the 1987 NHL draft," Wilkie says. "It was a promise we would never get to keep."

CHAPTER 6

Leesa's Ride

While the Swift Current Broncos played out the first half of their 1986–87 WHL season, Leesa Kraft was attending school in Moose Jaw. Originally from Penticton, British Columbia, she was a student at Aldersgate Bible College, a private school. She didn't attend Warriors games; she didn't know anything about the Broncos. In fact, she wasn't even close to being a hockey fan.

Near the end of December 1986, as most of the Broncos players headed home for Christmas, the twenty-one-year-old Kraft was on a Greyhound bus, en route to Penticton and Christmas with her family.

Prior to the 1800s, Penticton, located in British Columbia's south Okanagan, primarily was inhabited by the Salish, and the name Penticton means "a place to stay forever."

"It sure was a great place to grow up," Leesa Kraft — now Leesa Culp — says, adding that every time she returns for a vacation she wonders why she left. The eldest of three children, she grew up in a bungalow-style house on Toronto Avenue, alongside her mother, Sharon, and father, Len, and with sister Shawna and brother Trevor.

Len was a mechanic, and worked in the motorcycle shop — Kraft Cycle — operated by his father. So, as Leesa says, she grew up "knowing more about motorcycles, snowmobiles, hot rods, and race cars than I did about hockey."

One of her few experiences with hockey came in the early 1980s when she accompanied Shelley Webber, a high school friend, to a few British Columbia Hockey League games at Memorial Arena. Webber was dating Penticton Knights goaltender Norm Foster, who would go on to a fourteen-year professional career that included thirteen NHL games. (During his career, he would be teammates at one time or another with five of the 1986–87 Broncos: Tracy Egeland, Ian Herbers, Clarke Polglase, Peter Soberlak, and Bob Wilkie.)

During the eighteen-hour bus ride home for Christmas in 1986, Leesa had a lot of time to think about changes she was about to make in her life. She had met Bill Culp, a musician, and was planning a move to the Toronto area in order to be with him. As the bus sped west, she was trying to figure out just how she was going to break this news to her folks.

"I dreaded telling my family of my plans to move even farther away from home," she remembers. "My family was quite happy knowing I was living in a fairly sheltered environment surrounded by solid Christian influences on the Aldersgate campus. I wasn't sure how my parents would react to this move."

As she rationalized it at the time, "The idea of living in a big city excited me. It was a thrill to think I would be making a move to a part of the country about which I knew very little. I had gone from a sheltered home environment to a sheltered college environment, and I knew this move to Ontario would allow me to experience a lifestyle very unlike the one I'd had." But she knew there would be parental resistance.

"For this very reason, and the fact they had never met Bill, I knew my parents would be extremely reluctant to support this move," she says. "Knowing Bill was in a band put visions of a long-haired, tattooed, drug-smoking musician in my parents' heads. No amount of convincing otherwise was going to change their minds."

(In truth, Bill Culp had short hair, didn't have any tattoos, and didn't do drugs. From Dunnville, Ontario, he is the youngest of four children. His father, Herb, was the vice-president of the Dunnville Minor Sports Association and even coached minor hockey for a number of years. Bill's older brother Jamie played for Mount Royal College in Calgary and for the Dunnville Terriers, a junior C hockey team. In recent years, you may have seen Bill Culp on tour in "The Sun Records Show," a tribute that includes the music of Johnny Cash, Elvis Presley, Carl Perkins, and Jerry Lee Lewis.)

Shawna, Leesa's sister, had recently moved to Barrie, Ontario, in order to be closer to her future in-laws. So Leesa sold her parents on the move by telling them she would be closer to Shawna.

"I was sure my parents would find comfort in knowing I wouldn't be too many miles away from her if things didn't work out," Leesa says.

After Christmas, the plan was for Leesa to ride a bus back to Moose Jaw, where she would begin preparations for a January 20 flight from Regina to Toronto. However, in an effort to save some money, Leesa's parents suggested that she cash in her bus ticket and catch a ride with Mel Shepherd, a neighbour who drove a big rig back and forth between Penticton and Calgary. He would drop her off at the Calgary bus terminal and she would then take a Greyhound to Moose Jaw.

Never having been in a big rig, Leesa remembers it as "the biggest truck I had ever been in." She also remembers chatting with Mel and listening to 1980s pop songs like Glass Tiger's "Don't Forget Me When I'm Gone" as the trip began.

"Other than having to stop once to chain up before heading up a steep hill," she says, "it was a pretty uneventful drive."

That began to change as they approached Calgary. With the weather about to change for the worse, Mel told Leesa that he really wanted to unload his trailer, reload immediately, and head right back to Penticton. This meant he wouldn't be able to get her to the downtown bus terminal. Instead, he said, he knew a guy who was driving all the way to Montreal, and suggested they could hook up with him at the next truck stop. Essentially, Leesa would hitch a ride to Moose Jaw with another trucker, one she had never met.

She was apprehensive but, she says, "I figured Mel must think I'd be safe or he wouldn't suggest such an option."

Leesa and Mel grabbed a bite to eat at the truck stop, then got her luggage and headed for the other trucker's rig. That's when she saw the mural painted on the cab and immediately wondered if this was such a good idea.

Both sides of the glossy red cab of the truck were painted with an image of a scantily clad woman. Everything inside Leesa was screaming *Danger!* but her options were rather limited, so she clambered into the truck's cab.

They hit the road, and it wasn't long before the truck driver, a total stranger, started talking about the problems he was having with his wife. Which made Leesa think, "What trouble have I gotten myself into this time?"

Leesa knew exactly what was happening. A married, overweight veteran trucker was hitting on a naive college student. Attempting to let this guy know she wasn't available, Leesa mentioned "my boyfriend Bill" as often as possible.

And then, a few hours into what normally was an eight-hour run to Moose Jaw, the trucker chose to pull over, saying that he was going to get some sleep. It was in the middle of nowhere and traffic was minimal, but Leesa was thankful that it still was daylight.

As the trucker made his way to the back of the cab, where his bed was located, he told Leesa, "You should come back in the cab and get some sleep, too." Terrified, she clung to the door handle and wondered, *If I had to escape, what would I do? He would have all of my luggage and I'd be somewhere in Saskatchewan with nary a town in sight.*

About fifteen minutes later, the trucker climbed back into his seat. "I can't sleep if I know you're just sitting out here awake!" he said disgustedly. And just like that, they were back on the road to Moose Jaw.

By then, the snow and wind were increasing, and it wasn't long before the truck was caught in blizzard-like conditions. It may have been mid-afternoon, but it looked and felt more like early evening. It was in these conditions that they drove through Swift Current. As they reached the city's eastern edge, the trucker eased off the gas to allow a bus to merge in front of his rig. About five minutes later, the Trans-Canada Highway veered to the right a bit. The bus appeared to lose its grip and started to slide sideways.

With the bus slowing, the trucker geared down. Leesa and the trucker could only watch in disbelief as the rear end of the bus continued to slide down the steep roadside and into the ditch. Eventually, the bus fell over onto its right side. Then, after only a split second, it bounced right back up and continued to fly forward, still on the same steep angle.

Leesa remembers seeing things ejected out the windows, onto the road and into the ditch. At the time, she wondered, *Are those clothes flying out the windows?* Once they got closer to the bus, they realized it wasn't just clothes being tossed around like toothpicks in a storm — it was also people.

After several seconds of bone-jarring turbulence, the bus came to a crashing halt in the snowy ditch, again on its right side.

As the trucker pulled up beside the bus, he grabbed the handset for his CB and radioed for emergency assistance. Without further thought, he jumped out of the truck, yelling at Leesa, "Stay in the truck! Stay in the truck!"

There was no way she was going to stay in the truck. She climbed out and walked briskly around to the back of the bus.

"Suddenly," she recalls, "I noticed two boys...."

In her words: "Lying all alone, one boy — years later I would learn that it was Scott Kruger — was face down in the snowy grass, and the other was on his back. I didn't know much about emergency situations, but I knew you shouldn't move someone in case of neck or back injuries, so I chose to rush over to the boy who was on his back, and I knelt down. I was wearing a full-length, wool-tweed winter jacket, and was tempted to sit him up and wrap my coat around him.

"At the time, I felt a tremendous fear. Coming from a Free Methodist background, movies had been prohibited. I was twenty-one years of age and had seen only one scary movie in my life — *A Nightmare on Elm Street Part 2: Freddy's Revenge*. Although Bill found the movie disappointing, it had scared me silly. And now I think I was afraid that if I touched Trent [Kresse] he might make a sudden move and it would freak me out. I didn't reach down quickly and take his hand. I was hesitant, and I was trembling as I reached for his left hand. It was so much bigger than my own.

"His eyes were open, but sadly it was clear that I wasn't going to be able to do anything to help him. As I held his hand, I watched in horror as the colour of his face transformed from a pasty white to a stony shade of blue. I had never felt so helpless. I kept thinking that maybe if I knew how to perform CPR — something, anything — I would be able to help. But it was too late. As I stood up and stepped back, a man approached and started to perform CPR on the boy whom I had been kneeling beside."

Leesa then took a moment to glance around. "It was then when I noticed the unimaginable — there were two more bodies trapped under the bus," she says.

With the bus on its side and the front door inaccessible, the trucker helped the remaining players and passengers out through the shattered windshield. The survivors began collecting themselves. They were looking around to see if everyone was okay. All around her, Leesa could hear moaning and crying, and people calling out for each other. She just stood there in disbelief.

It wasn't until almost twenty-one years later that Leesa learned that it was the Swift Current Broncos whose bus she had watched crash. In 1986, she didn't follow hockey, nor did she hang out with anyone who did.

One morning in January 2007, a headline on Yahoo! — "Fifth Teen Dies from Injuries in Meaford Crash" — practically leapt off her computer screen and caused flashbacks. The story chronicled an accident that had occurred on a wet, slushy highway and claimed the lives of five teenage hockey players. That was enough to awaken memories that had been mostly dormant for more than twenty years.

And so it was that Leesa Culp, who had watched in agony as the Broncos' bus crashed, finally began to learn about what she had witnessed. She started by doing a Web search for "Swift Current bus accident 1986." That led her to Brian Costello.

By then, Costello was with *The Hockey News*. In 1986, he had been in his second year as a sports writer with the *Swift Current Sun* and had been sitting at the front of the bus. Costello, who suffered cuts and bruises in the crash, told Leesa that he distinctly remembers hearing the trucker's call for help before he was helped out of the bus.

Aid started to arrive within minutes, and the trucker, anxious to get back on the road, came looking for Leesa. Obviously in shock, she felt only numbness as she climbed back into the truck.

"I was confused and scared and wondering what I had just seen," she says. "I couldn't stop thinking about holding the hand of that boy in the field. My eyes were filled with tears, but I could still see his face etched clearly in my mind."

That boy turned out to be Trent Kresse, who was one of the Broncos' leaders.

Courtesy of Leesa Culp.

Leesa Culp and Bob Wilkie, meeting for the first time in May 2007. Wilkie was living in Hershey, Pennsylvania, at the time.

"I came to suspect that it had been Trent from a picture I found on the Internet," Leesa says. "His eyes struck me right away. But it wasn't until my first conversation with Brian Costello that I knew for sure. Brian was able to tell me right away from my description of the scene."

After leaving the scene, Leesa and the trucker rolled through the ugly weather, getting closer and closer to Moose Jaw. It was a quiet ride as driver and passenger found themselves lost in their own thoughts.

"I couldn't shake the picture of Trent's twisted body from my mind," Leesa says. "He was lying on his back and I walked around and took his left hand, which was straight and flat on the ground. One leg was twisted at the knee and I just knew that it didn't look right."

As she stared into the darkness, with the snow pounding against the truck's windshield, she wondered if maybe it all had been a dream … or a nightmare. It also struck Leesa that she was all alone. Her parents were two provinces away. Her boyfriend was across the country. Her friends were at home for the holidays with their families. And she was in a transport truck with a stranger who had tried to hit on her.

When they reached the outskirts of Moose Jaw, she got out of the truck at Rodo's, the same twenty-four-hour truck stop where she and Bill had had their first date. It was dark — Leesa remembers thinking that this was the darkest night she had ever experienced — as she gathered her luggage and located a pay phone. Desperately wanting to hear a familiar voice, she called her apartment. Her roommates weren't home, and she wasn't interested in going home to an empty apartment. She then thought of Stuart McIver, a college friend, and phoned his house, but his dad said he was away for a couple of days. Somehow — maybe it was the tremor in Leesa's voice — Mr. McIver sensed something was wrong.

Leesa tried to tell him what had happened, but it was a struggle. Finally it all came out. She told him what she had witnessed and where she was, and that she needed someone to pick her up. It wasn't long before he was at Rodo's and they were on the way to the McIver home. Mrs. McIver sat Leesa down in the living room and asked if she wanted to talk about what happened. After hearing the details, she suggested Leesa call home.

"Who wouldn't want to talk to Mom after what had just happened?" Leesa says, admitting that there were times when she felt like a six-year-old badly in need of a mother's hug.

However, the first two times she called and spoke to her mother, Leesa cried so hard that she was unable to speak, and had to hang up. Eventually, she calmed down and was able to explain things to her mother.

Leesa found she was completely exhausted. Recognizing this, Mrs. McIver led her to a vacant bedroom and suggested that she get as much rest as she needed. After the worst day of her life, Leesa finally climbed into bed. But it took a long, long time for her to fall asleep. As she says, "I was afraid to close my eyes."

Even today, her memories of the first few days after the bus accident are a blur. She thinks she must have heard something about the accident on the news at some point prior to leaving Moose Jaw for Toronto, but says she doesn't remember talking or even thinking about the accident.

"I didn't realize it then," she says, "but I was burying the memory and pain of the accident ... I was in survival mode."

She spent New Year's Eve with friends in Moose Jaw, although she didn't want to be there. In fact, twenty years later, she got together with two Moose Jaw friends, Yvonne Scancen and Murray Schock, on the occasion of Murray's fortieth birthday.

"I had put together a scrapbook of pictures from our college days, and I had some pictures near the end of the scrapbook of the 1986 New Year's Eve party," Leesa says. Looking at the photos, she said to Murray, "I don't know whose party this was, but I remember not wanting to be there."

Murray replied: "That was my party!"

"I felt like such a heel for saying what I did," Leesa now says, "but I had been in no mood to party on December 31, 1986."

CHAPTER 7

The Invisible Goaltenders

Artie Feher and Bob Crockett. Call them the invisible goaltenders. They were in Swift Current, and then they weren't.

Feher, who had celebrated his twentieth birthday on September 21, 1986, was on the Swift Current Broncos' ill-fated bus slightly more than three months later. But it seemed few people were aware of his presence. Feher had arrived in Swift Current with little fanfare; he would leave the same way.

Crockett wasn't on the bus. His name, however, was on a list of survivors that appeared in the *Swift Current Sun*. Neither would play even one minute for the Broncos.

In September 1986, Artie Feher was fighting to keep his WHL career alive. A six-foot-one, 170-pound native of Prince Albert, his WHL career had already included stints with the Saskatoon Blades (six games), Brandon Wheat Kings (fifty-five), and Moose Jaw Warriors (eight), all of those appearances having been made over the previous two seasons.

When teams went to training camps in August 1986, Feher was with the Warriors. They released him — each WHL team is allowed to keep a maximum of three twenty-year-olds, and he got caught up in what is an annual numbers game in major junior hockey — and found himself with the Spokane Chiefs. The Chiefs would use thirty-nine different players that season; Feher was one of four goaltenders who got into action. He played in six games, Bill Francione got into ten, and John Colvin played in twenty-nine. Future NHLer Troy Gamble was the workhorse, playing in thirty-eight. In November, when the Chiefs decided to go with Gamble and Colvin, Feher again found himself without a WHL team to call his own.

"In the middle of November I was released, yet I didn't want to leave Spokane," says Feher, who is now known as Art and is the principal of Red Wing School, an elementary school in Prince Albert. "I found a part-time job laying carpet and thought my playing days were over."

He was wrong. Like so many players before and after him, Feher found that the game of hockey had a real hold on him. As much as he knew he likely should walk away and get on with his life, he simply couldn't cut the tie that binds. So when his phone rang early in December, he answered. Rob Daum, the head coach of the Saskatchewan Junior Hockey League's Nipawin Hawks, was on the other end. The Hawks needed a goaltender — was Feher interested?

It didn't take Feher long to agree to join the Hawks, who play in the junior A SJHL, which is one level below the WHL.

"It was a large curve going from Spokane to Nipawin," Feher says, "but I still wanted to play ... so I went."

Feher wasn't in Nipawin long when his phone rang again. Another team was looking for a goaltender.

"Graham James called and asked me to come to Swift Current," Feher says. "I said I needed time to think about it because I had committed to play in Nipawin."

By now, it was into the middle of December, and teams were preparing for the Christmas break. Feher told James that he would think about the offer over Christmas.

"I took a couple of days to think about it over the holidays," Feher says, "and I decided to go. So I said goodbye to Nipawin — I believe it was on December 28 — and left for Swift Current."

The decision really wasn't that tough. As a twenty-year-old, Feher knew he was in his last season of junior hockey. This was it — his last shot. And at least a part of him was still chasing the dream. So would he want to finish his junior career in the Saskatchewan junior league? Or in the WHL, a league that is one step below the professional ranks, a league in which he previously had played, and one in which he felt he definitely could play? Like so many athletes in his situation, he felt it was simply a matter of getting himself into the right place at the right time.

The Broncos, in their first season back in Swift Current, had been juggling goaltenders — by season's end, they would use five of them in games — and had not yet found a combination with which they were comfortable. So why wouldn't Feher roll the dice one more time?

When Feher arrived in Swift Current, he discovered that the team, whose players were just rolling back into town from the Christmas break, didn't have a billet for him.

"I ended up in a hotel that night with another player, whose name I don't remember," Feher recalls. "We practised on December 28 and 29 and left for Regina on December 30."

Feher boarded the bus to Regina that fateful day knowing he wouldn't play against the Pats that night. In fact, he was so sure that his services wouldn't be required that he left his hockey equipment in the Broncos' dressing room.

"I was just along for the trip and to watch the team play; to familiarize myself with the players, at least a bit," he says. Still, the happenings of that day are as clear in his mind now as his wedding day or the births of his children.

"Before getting to the rink, I went to McDonald's for a bite to eat and brought it onto the bus," he says. "As we pulled out of Swift Current, I finished my lunch. I took off my coat and put it up in one of the top racks. I was sitting right in the middle of the bus on the right-hand side in a window seat. There was nobody beside me. Trevor Kruger and Kurt Lackten were sitting across from me." Kruger was one of the Broncos' goaltenders; Lackten, a rugged forward, was the team captain.

Feher remembers that he was just getting settled into his seat when "the bus driver yelled 'Hold on!'" Feher says. "The first reaction I had was to grab the seat in front of me and look up to see what was going on. I could tell the bus driver had lost control of the bus as we began to fishtail. We ended up in the ditch when we hit the farm approach.

"As we hit, all the windows in the bus shattered. I saw a 'Do Not Enter' sign that had been on the shoulder of the highway; it was lying in the aisle of the bus.

"I can't remember if we landed on the other side of the approach and the bus flipped onto its right side, or if the bus twisted in the air as it hit the approach and became airborne and then landed on its right side. But we slid in the ditch, and I remember grabbing on to the seat for all it was worth. That is the only thing that kept me inside the bus because my right knee now was sticking through the broken windows and dragging along the ground."

Feher also remembers, almost in slow motion, what it was like when the bus came grinding to a halt.

"As the bus came to a stop, it was very eerie," he says. "The wind was whistling through it and not a sound from the bus was heard. Then, after what seemed like an eternity, someone from the back of the bus began yelling to get help and to get a doctor.

"Trevor and Kurt were lying on top of me, and I remember Kurt getting up very fast and going to the front of the bus."

Lackten helped people get off the bus — they had to exit through the hole where the windshield had been. The bus had come to rest on its right side, thus the front door was inaccessible.

"Players began to scream," Feher says. "I didn't know what was happening."

By now, people in other vehicles were arriving at the accident site on the Trans-Canada Highway.

"I remember someone saying that we should all get into a car and meet at the hospital," Feher says. "As I left the bus and walked to a car — there were many of them now stopped at the side of the road — I looked at the bus and saw two groups of people behind it. I instantly knew there were two players back there, but I didn't know the extent of their injuries."

To this day, Feher doesn't recall who gave him a ride to the hospital. And it wasn't until after he got to the hospital that he began to understand the seriousness of the accident.

"As the players began to gather, we heard of players being thrown out of the bus and being trapped," he says. Feher especially was concerned about the status of Trent Kresse, the only player on the Broncos with whom he was familiar. The two had played together with the SJHL's Lloydminster Lancers in 1982–83.

"When it really hit me that this was serious was when we saw Scott and Trevor's mom come into the hospital," Feher says. "She was wearing pins and buttons — the typical hockey mom and fan. I was with a group of players when a doctor approached Mrs. Kruger, who was about ten metres away from us. As the doctor [spoke with her], she broke down, and all of us sat in the chairs and stared."

The doctor and Broncos assistant coach Lorne Frey, who was Louise Kruger's brother, informed her and her husband, Walt, that their son, Scott, had been killed in the crash. Having witnessed that, Feher began to realize how serious the accident in which he had just been involved actually was. At the same time, he began to understand that it soon would be major news. Perhaps it was also the shock wearing off, but it dawned on him that he should call his parents and let them know that he was okay. He didn't want them to hear about it and wonder about his status.

"I phoned my parents in Prince Albert to let them know that there was a serious bus accident, that there were lives lost, but I was okay," he remembers. "I also called the Nipawin Hawks to let them know as well."

Feher was then checked over by a doctor, who found him to have "a badly bruised [right] kneecap." Feher was given a pair of crutches to help him keep the weight off the injured knee.

"As I began to leave the hospital," he says, "we were given instructions to meet at the rink the next day." But before he could even think about the following day, Feher had to find a place to spend the night. After what he had been through, going back to a hotel didn't particularly appeal to him. As things turned out, he didn't have to spend another night in the hotel.

"Tim Tisdale and his parents offered me a place to stay for the night," Feher says. "I don't think I ever thanked them for that."

Defenceman Jason Proulx also stayed with Feher in the warmth of the Tisdale home that night. Proulx, who had been acquired with Peter Soberlak from the Kamloops Blazers early in the season, ended up staying with the Tisdales for the duration of the season.

By the time the Tisdales, Feher, and Proulx got settled, the media was onto the story and television news crews had footage for their newscasts. It was while Feher was at the Tisdales' home that he saw the first pictures.

"We saw the news and the footage of the bus and couldn't believe what had just happened," Feher says. He found it almost incomprehensible that he had been involved in what he was seeing on television. Despite the horrors he had just experienced, he adds, "I remember, surprisingly, that I had a pretty good night's sleep that night."

When he awoke the morning of December 31, all kinds of questions were rushing through Feher's mind. After all, he had joined the Broncos just a couple of days earlier. Heck, he hadn't even gotten into a game with them.

"What is going to happen now?" he remembers wondering. "Are we going to play again? How long will it be?"

Before long, Feher decided that no matter what the immediate future held for Swift Current, he wouldn't be part of it. He decided that he was going back to Nipawin.

"I never really knew anyone on that bus, besides Trent," he explains, "so I decided that since I really wasn't part of the team, I was going to leave. I went to the rink to talk to Graham James and he was very supportive. I noticed he had a lot of cuts on his face.

"Since I wasn't part of the team, I didn't want to take part in all the aftermath that was to follow. I said I was going back to Nipawin to finish my junior hockey career. Having said all that, Graham never tried to keep me. He said whatever I wanted to do, I could do. I picked up my equipment and got into my car." Had Feher stayed with the Broncos, he would have been one of three goaltenders, along with Trevor Kruger and Pat Nogier.

As James told the *Swift Current Sun*, "It would have been tough for him here being the third goalie. [It would have been] very difficult to fit in. I understand how he feels."

Before leaving Swift Current, Feher made one stop.

"I decided to go to the RCMP building to see if I could go back to the bus and pick up my suit coat," he says, referring to the coat that he had placed on the top shelf before making himself comfortable in his seat. "They were reluctant, but an officer took me in his police car to a Quonset [hut] out of town where the bus was parked."

Feher never will forget what he saw in that hut.

"It was unbelievable," he says. "Glass everywhere ... dirt, straw, and a bus that looked like twisted metal. I was allowed to enter the bus to get my coat. I walked over to the 'Do Not Enter' sign and retrieved my coat." As it turned out, the coat was in such poor shape that it no longer was wearable.

"The officer drove me back to my car and off I went," Feher says.

Three days and a lifetime worth of experiences after arriving in Swift Current, and without playing even one minute for the Broncos, Feher was headed back to Nipawin.

On his way out of Swift Current, he stopped at the accident site.

"All you could see was the slide marks of the bus and a few playing cards scattered around," he recalls. "I started to drive with my left foot, as my right leg was now in pain, and I went to Moose Jaw to see my old billets and we talked about the accident. From there, it was off to Prince Albert. I arrived at my parents' house around 10:00 p.m."

It was New Year's Eve, but Feher wasn't in a mood to celebrate. Instead, he went right to bed. He simply couldn't get enough sleep, he found.

Feher rejoined the Hawks a few days later and finished the season with them, playing in thirty-four games. In fact, he is right there in the team photo, seated second from right in the front row. There are two other goaltenders — Dean Ross and Jeff Holness — in the photo. Feher received one of the team's individual awards, for most gentlemanly player.

Because he didn't feel part of the Broncos, Feher says he wouldn't have felt comfortable attending the memorial service on January 4 in Swift Current. Ten years later, he received a call from *The Hockey News*. They were doing a story on the accident and were preparing a where-are-they-now story as part of the package. He also heard from CBC Radio.

"They called and I told my story to them," he says. "But they didn't air the story because right after that the Sheldon Kennedy story broke."

On January 2, 1997, Graham James pleaded guilty to 350 sexual assaults: three hundred on Kennedy, and fifty on an unidentified player.

When Feher was with the Broncos, few people were aware that he was even there. And even ten years after the fact, his story wasn't told, pre-empted by another story.

Indeed, Feher was an invisible Bronco.

So, too, was Bob Crockett, who had been scheduled to be on the Broncos' bus for that trip to Regina. However, he didn't make it.

Born in Pitt Meadows, British Columbia, Crockett was two months past his sixteenth birthday during Christmas 1986. He had been the property of the Lethbridge Broncos, so his rights went to Swift Current when the franchise was sold to John Rittinger and his group. Crockett had been in a couple of Lethbridge training camps prior to reporting to Swift Current in the fall of 1986.

"In Lethbridge," he remembers, "I was a highly touted goalie — but in Swift Current they didn't know who I was. I knew I had potential, but I had to prove myself all over again."

Graham James, the Broncos' general manager and head coach, would spend much of the 1986–87 season's first half searching for a dependable goaltender. It wouldn't be Bob Crockett.

"I was sent home right after main camp, and I was brought back a few weeks later," Crockett recalls. "But I never got to play and prove myself. I guess Graham had his reasons.... I don't think Graham knew what he wanted in a goalie."

As Christmas approached, Crockett made plans to return to British Columbia's Lower Mainland, where he would spend the holidays with his family. He knew Joe Sakic — a Burnaby, British Columbia, native — from Lethbridge training camps and from Sakic's minor hockey career on the Lower Mainland. So Crockett caught a ride with Sakic to Calgary, and the two of them flew west to spend some holiday time with their families.

When it came time to return to Swift Current, however, Crockett missed his flight because, he said, he "was delayed at home." In the end, he chose not to go back at all. Instead, he played for the junior B Burnaby Bluehawks of the West Coast junior league.

Still, when the *Swift Current Sun* printed a list of accident survivors, Crockett's name somehow ended up on it, although he wasn't even in the city. According to Crockett, when some people heard reports of a sixteen-year-old having died in the bus crash, they thought it was him. Of course, it would turn out to have been forward Brent Ruff.

Crockett learned of the accident from his girlfriend's parents. At first, he says, he didn't believe the news. And then he became quite upset — after all, these were his buddies. He may not have been a part of the Broncos, but he had spent some time with them and he knew most of the players. He was, he says, particularly fond of Chris Mantyka. Crockett remembers Mantyka weighing in for training camp.

"I remember thinking, *Who's that Fu Manchu? He'll never make it.* But then Chris got on the ice and kicked the snot out of three guys. Off the ice, he was the nicest guy." Crockett also remembers Mantyka's trademark: "He would put his elbow pads on loose so that if he got into a fight he could easily pull them off and throw them at his opponent, and while his opponent was trying to pull them off his face to see, he could beat the guy up."

Even though Crockett never played for the Broncos, he remembers the feeling he got from being part of the team, even for such a brief time.

"They were superheroes," he says. "The whole community loved them. The high-school students all had Broncos binders ... and even the third-string goalie was a star."

Crockett returned to the Broncos for training camp in August 1987 but, by his own admission, he was thirty pounds overweight. For one reason or another, Crockett never would play in the WHL. He says he had opportunities to play with junior teams in Richmond and Merritt, British Columbia, among others, but always said no because he was trying to understand how he had gone from being "highly touted" to this.

In the end, just when he thought his career was over, Crockett joined the Williams Lake Mustangs of the Peace Cariboo junior league. It was Pat McGill, an uncle of Swift Current defenceman Ryan McGill, who convinced Crockett to keep playing. Pat was coaching the Mustangs and said he needed a goaltender. Crockett reported and sat for two weeks until, he says, an injury took out another goaltender. Given an opportunity, Crockett played and played and played, even helping the Mustangs to a league championship in 1988–89.

But when he was done with the Mustangs after his twenty-year-old season, Crockett was done with hockey. While with the Mustangs, he proved to himself that he "could be a good goalie, and that was enough for me."

He never played again, and says he has no regrets.

When asked about the Broncos and Graham James, and what they were able to accomplish after the crash, including winning the 1989 Memorial Cup, Crockett replies, "Graham had help putting the team together. There were other scouts. It wasn't all him."

Now in his early forties, Crockett lives in Maple Ridge, British Columbia, with his son, Luke, and works for Avcorp Industries, a company based in nearby Delta that designs and builds airframe structures for aircraft manufacturers.

CHAPTER 8

Sober's Story

Bob Wilkie spent the evening of December 30, 1986, in hospital. The Swift Current Broncos defenceman wasn't going anywhere, and the way he felt, he really couldn't think of a place he would rather be.

While he and team captain Kurt Lackten shared a hospital room, many of their teammates ended up at the home of Colleen and Frank MacBean. Sheldon Kennedy, Joe Sakic, and Dan Lambert billeted with the MacBeans.

Frank was a local lawyer who found time to serve on the Broncos' board of directors. He had been involved with the numerous attempts to bring a WHL franchise back to Swift Current. Colleen was an English and history teacher and guidance counsellor at Swift Current Comprehensive, a local high school.

The players who showed up sat in the MacBeans' basement and cried and laughed and cried and laughed some more. They were awake until the early hours of December 31 as they tried to make at least some sense of what had happened, trying to understand how it was that four teammates had been killed in the crash of their team bus just a few short hours earlier.

Of all the places to be in Swift Current, the MacBean home likely was the best place for everyone, considering the circumstances. Colleen and

Rod Steensland.

Sheldon Kennedy (left), Joe Sakic, and Danny Lambert, sporting Cooperalls.

Frank had first become billets when a hockey friend of their son Nick's needed a place to stay. The MacBeans would go on to provide a second home to more than forty players. But most importantly, if anyone knew the trauma these Broncos players — all of them teenagers, most of them away from home for the first time — were going through, it was Colleen and Frank. Not only was Colleen a guidance counsellor, but she and Frank had been through the tragedy of losing two of their sons in an automobile accident. Kevin and David, both of whom had been adopted and were just thirteen years of age, had been killed two years earlier.

Colleen said of the night of the bus accident, "Many of them just huddled up right here on the floor, staring off into an unknown future, while Frank and I simply listened. We listened to their passions, their dreams … and encouraged them to do what the guys would have wanted them to do: finish the season, be positive and reach for their goals."

Colleen would later be honoured with the WHL's Distinguished Service Award, in 2006. This award is presented annually to an individual associated with the league who has made an extraordinary contribution over an extended period of time. But on the night of December 30, 1986, it was Frank who said "Life must go on," and how true that was.

One of the players huddled in the MacBeans' basement on that blustery night was Peter Soberlak, who had been acquired from the Kamloops Blazers earlier in the season. Soberlak doesn't remember a lot about what he refers to as "post-accident," but he remembers being in the MacBeans' home. And he remembers a New Year's Eve party in someone else's home the next night, only because Darren and Trevor Kruger, whose brother Scott had been killed, were there.

At the time, Soberlak wasn't far removed from being considered the best player in his age group in the West, if not all of Canada. But, unknown to anyone but Soberlak, he was struggling with his own demons. Soberlak was only seventeen, but he was quickly losing his love for the game and he knew it. He just wasn't sure how to deal with it.

And now, on top of that, he was in an unfamiliar home, trying to understand what had happened to him and his friends only a few hours before.

In the aftermath of the accident, grief counsellors were never provided for the players or anyone else in the organization. In Sheldon Kennedy's book, *Why I Didn't Say Anything,* which was published in 2006, Kennedy writes that he suspects general manager and head coach Graham James rejected counselling for the team members in an effort to prevent anyone from finding out about the abuse to which he was subjecting Kennedy.

Courtesy of Leesa Culp.

Bob Wilkie and Colleen MacBean in July 2007.

"You would have thought that someone in charge would have arranged for the survivors to receive therapy to help them deal with the shock and grief following the accident," Kennedy writes, "but none of us received any kind of professional help. Nobody seemed to want to talk about what had happened....

"So how did we deal with the tragedy? We got back to our lives and tried to move on. We played hockey. And, as men are prone to do, we drank. Only after a few beers, or more than a few, could we talk about how the crash made us feel. Some of us wondered why we had survived while others died. We were plagued by a lot of what ifs."

Everyone — players and staff alike — was left to deal with their grief alone or with each other.

Soberlak, who was seated on the bus in close proximity to the four players who died, says, "We had nobody to deal with — nobody to talk to or turn to — other than my parents on the phone." At the time, Soberlak says, the fact that counselling wasn't made available wasn't seen as a big deal, at least not to him.

"It didn't seem strange to me because everything I'd gone through in Kamloops and Swift Current ... really, I had to suck it up myself anyway,"

Soberlak says. "I could tell my folks and they would always be supportive, but they didn't know … they had no idea the stuff that went on."

As a fifteen-year-old playing in Kamloops, Soberlak was seen by scouts as a wonderfully talented player. The following season, he joined his hometown Blazers. But what should have been the start of a promising career was actually the beginning of the end.

"My sixteen-year-old year shaped the way I felt about hockey," he says. "In order to be a pro, you have to live it right through to your bones. After that season, there was a drastic change in my love for the game."

There were many times when Soberlak found himself thinking, *This isn't what I thought it was going to be.* Today, in his early forties, with a wife and child, Soberlak is the chairperson of physical education at Thompson Rivers University in Kamloops. He has a bachelor of arts in psychology, with a minor in sociology, from the University of British Columbia, and a master's degree in sport and exercise psychology from Queen's University in Kingston, Ontario. And now, when he looks back, he is especially proud of one thing in his junior hockey career.

"I'm proud that I stuck it out — fought through it," he says.

His stint with his hometown Blazers should have been a proud time for him. Having the opportunity to play in front of family and friends should have been a real thrill. It wasn't.

"It was really horrible," he says. "In a lot of cases, I feared going on the bus, feared going on road trips … just because of the humiliation and constant verbal abuse. And then the physical abuse in practice.… I remember trying to do a practice drill [with Kamloops] and [one veteran player] swinging his stick as hard as he could at me and slashing me. If I try to fight him, what am I going to do? I got eighteen guys wanting to kick the shit out of me because I'm a sixteen-year-old hotshot hometown boy."

There was more, too. There was hazing and what Soberlak says was physical abuse.

"What I went through in Kamloops destroyed my confidence," he says. "I can deal with that now, but it was just horrific for me. It sucked the life out of me … I was physically assaulted." The anguish in his expression is painful to witness as he recalls what he went through as a sixteen-year-old.

"You think I have not suffered — have not had repercussions from what I went through there — serious, absolutely long-term, continuous major repercussions of what happened to me in that situation. I guarantee you I have."

Those were the days when a lot of coaches felt they had to break down players completely and then build them up. That wasn't going to work with Soberlak, who admits that the treatment he received in Kamloops broke his spirit and destroyed his love for the game.

"That's the only thing I am bitter about in my hockey career," Soberlak says. "My first year in Kamloops … it was the worst year of my life."

Still, he stayed in the game until he was twenty-three years of age. As he says, "I slugged it out for three years in the minors." Eventually, he ended up in camp with the Philadelphia Flyers. It was the autumn of 1992. Soberlak had broken an ankle while with the Broncos — it was during a game in Calgary — and was starting to realize that he would never be healthy.

"I'm coming back into my own zone," he recalls of the game in which he was injured. "I curl through the middle of the ice. Wilkie or Darren Kruger fired a beautiful pass up on my stick. I one-touch it across the ice and Joe [Sakic] picks it up and goes down and scores. In the meantime, as I deflected that puck, who's coming right at me to run me from the other side of the ice but the biggest guy I've ever seen on skates, Mark Tinordi. My leg gets caught between a checker from behind and him coming through.

"I'm sitting on the ice and they're all saying, 'Get up.' I know my leg is busted. It was busted in my skate."

Were that injury to occur today, there is no doubt but that Soberlak would undergo surgery and by the following season would be as good as new. But that's not the way it was in the spring of 1987.

"There was talk of me having surgery," Soberlak says, "but all I got out of Graham [James] with the doctors was, 'We've got to get it in a cast because he has to be back for playoffs.'"

There wasn't any cast and there weren't any playoffs for Soberlak. He would never again be the superb skater he had been.

"There was an NHL scout, I think for Buffalo, who was there that night, and a few years later he said to my dad, 'Peter was never the same after that injury,'" Soberlak says. "And he was right."

Soberlak came out of it with one leg slightly longer than the other. "It just got worse and worse," he says. He had taken power skating from the age of four, he had been a figure skater, and now he couldn't edge properly, couldn't take off properly.

"I was just never the same skater," he says. "Even [Kamloops head coach Ken Hitchcock] and those guys said I was probably the best seventeen-year-old in the country. And I was. But I was never, ever the same skater."

The injury occurred during his draft season. While it had been speculated that he might go early in the first round, he was taken twenty-first overall by the Edmonton Oilers.

"Right before the draft," he says, "I was getting all kinds of phone calls. 'How's your leg? Is your leg okay?' I was rated higher in the first round; I thought I was going to go higher."

He ended up with the Oilers' AHL affiliate, the Cape Breton Oilers, who played out of Sydney. He had twenty-three points in sixty games his first season and thirty-six in seventy games in 1990–91. The next season, he played in only twenty-two games.

"It was a tough one because a lot of people didn't understand," he says. "I would say to them, 'Now my back is getting sore, my groins are sore.'" Trying to compensate for his leg meant he was beginning to struggle with hip and back problems.

During the summer of 1992, he had surgery on his foot in Vancouver and then walked on with Philadelphia.

"In my last stint in Philadelphia," he remembers, "I almost made the Flyers … if my injury hadn't been bad I would have had a good chance."

Still, Soberlak says, his stint in Philly's camp was the "most exciting part of what I thought was going to be my pro career." The Flyers wanted to sign him to a two-way contract — meaning one salary in the NHL and a much lower stipend in the AHL. He says he told then–Flyers general manager Russ Farwell that "it was one-way or I don't play." Soberlak adds, "I wasn't going to play in the American league anymore. I wasn't going to play for thirty-five grand and fight.…"

There was one chapter left in Soberlak's hockey career. He signed to play with Canada's national team under head coach Tom Renney.

"I went there for about a month, but it just wasn't getting any better physically," Soberlak says. "I couldn't edge or turn properly."

And so one morning in the autumn of 1992, Soberlak woke up and admitted to himself that it was over. The guy who just eight years earlier was perhaps the best fifteen-year-old hockey player in Canada was finished, without having played even one NHL game.

"I just woke up, packed up my stuff, and drove home. And that was it," he says. "I still remember driving from Calgary thinking, *I'm done, I'm not going back, what the hell am I going to do with my life now?*" He also says he felt "huge relief."

"Huge relief that I had actually committed to myself and that I had decided," he says. "A huge relief ... a huge sense of freedom and relief."

From the age of eighteen or nineteen, he says, "I had played without enjoying it, not really having fun with the game." Looking back, Soberlak says his future as a hockey player was determined when he was sixteen years of age. It was a season during which he totalled twenty-one points, ten of them goals, in fifty-five games with the Blazers. Then, as he would now were he playing, he heard a lot about mental toughness.

These days, Soberlak also works in the area of sports psychology and has addressed WHL players about that very thing.

"What is mental toughness? You have to be mentally tough. What the hell does that mean?" Soberlak says. Then he provides the answer: "You have to be self-confident. Nobody can break you."

He pauses and thinks back to 1985–86.

"Ken Hitchcock, his coaching staff, his veteran players ... they broke me," he says. "I never rebuilt myself from that."

A handful of games into his second WHL season, Soberlak was dealt to Swift Current. At first, he was relieved because he was going to get a new start. It wasn't long before he found out that wasn't going to happen.

"I thought it couldn't have been worse than it was in Kamloops, but it was," he says. "It wasn't worse for me [as a player], but the whole context and culture of it was worse."

He kept telling himself to give it time; that things would get better. "That was always the underlying thought: it's going to get better," he says. He kept trying to convince himself that "I just have to get through this next thing and then it's all going to be great, I'm going to be a great pro and I'm going to have a great life."

That never happened, of course. The bus accident, he says, helped push him in the direction he eventually took.

"I was absolutely headed that way and this gave it a good nudge," he says.

Sadly, after he left the game, he found that he didn't miss it. Not at all. There were things he missed, but the game wasn't one of them.

"What I really missed, and what I still miss, is the guys," he says. "I miss the dressing room, I miss the guys, I miss the hotels, I miss the dinners. I didn't miss the game at all."

What about the injuries? "That's a minor piece of why I didn't continue to play," he responds.

During his playing career, he never did confide in his parents. He never did attempt to unburden himself. He never tried to tell them that he no longer loved the game of hockey. He never said a word, despite the fact that his father, John, was a well-known minor hockey coach in Kamloops.

"If I had told them, they likely would have believed me and got me out of there," Soberlak says. "But in that context you suck it up and you turn it inside and you deal with it. Some guys deal with it in different ways and, unfortunately, some deal with it with drugs and alcohol."

Soberlak dealt with it, as he says, by "sucking it up."

"To this day," he says, "I'm proud of the fact I stuck it out and even got through those situations. I held my head up ... what it affected later on was my love for the game. I didn't love it anymore and therefore I wasn't successful."

During his struggles with the game of hockey, music may well have kept Soberlak together. He had long played guitar, but he didn't really get serious about it until the early 1990s when he was in Cape Breton. From that point on, he always had a guitar with him.

Today, he will tell you, "Music is my number one — that's my love. That is my passion in life. That was the difference between hockey at that point. I loved music. I'll always love it."

Later, he would play Billy Miner, the legendary bank robber, in a touristy stage production that involved two shows a night, three nights a week, for eight months of the year. He did this while working full-time at Thompson Rivers University.

He's been in bands — he admits a band can be a substitute for a team — and he writes songs. "Music is something I have always loved," Soberlak says. "It's in my blood, whereas hockey wasn't the same. There's not the same emotional connection.

"I couldn't survive having to be intense and mean and aggressive ... I just couldn't do it. It was work for me from the time I was sixteen."

Understand that at the age of sixteen, Soberlak may have been the prototype for the perfect hockey player. He was big, he was strong, he could skate, he could shoot, and he was tough — when he had to be.

"I did it ... I think the [Regina] *Leader-Post* rated me one of the top five fighters in the Eastern Division one time," he says, with a rueful chuckle. "I could fight but I didn't want to. I didn't like it. That just wasn't me." He did it out of self-preservation.

"That was the worst mistake I made," he says now. "I clobbered a few guys and it was like, 'Why aren't you doing this all the time?' But I didn't play hockey so I could punch guys in the face. Some guys can do that, and good for them. I just can't."

About twenty years after watching teammate Chris Mantyka die underneath the overturned Broncos' bus, Peter Soberlak sat down and wrote "Secrets Safe with Me," a song that is included on the Pete Soberlak Band's *Thrill of the Chase* CD. To hear Soberlak sing the chorus to "Secrets Safe with Me" is to hear a young man still trying to come to grips with that December day in 1986. Here, courtesy of Soberlak, are the lyrics to "Secrets Safe with Me":

> Sometimes you feel your life is a moment
> Disguised by all you felt it could be.
> Hold tight, no more dreams in the window.
> Goodbye, your secret's safe with me.
>
> Can you hear me calling out for you?
> Can you see me reaching out? There's nothing I can do,

And I know that I left there without you.
Goodbye, your secret's safe with me.

Sometimes you feel your life is a moment,
A flash of light, it changes instantly.
Hold tight, no more dreams in the window.
Goodbye, your secret's safe with me.

Can you hear me calling out for you?
Can you see me reaching out? There's nothing I can do,
And I know that I left there without you.
Goodbye, your secret's safe with me.

You keep coming back into my life
Ever since the day we said goodbye, and if I said to you

Can you hear me calling out for you?
Can you see me reaching out? There's nothing I can do,
And I know that I left there without you.
Goodbye, your secret's safe …
Goodbye, your secret's safe …
Goodbye, your secret's safe with me.

CHAPTER 9

Saying Goodbye

Following the accident involving the Swift Current Broncos' bus, WHL officials met in Calgary. They had to work on scheduling a memorial service and, as ugly as it may have seemed, they had to decide when the Broncos would return to game action.

A decision was made to postpone four games, which would give the Broncos' management and players — and their fans — an opportunity to grieve, to attend funerals, and to catch their breath.

Players were told they could return to their homes for a day or two, but they were asked to return for a memorial service that was to be held January 4 in the Broncos' home arena, the Centennial Civic Centre.

Defenceman Bob Wilkie went home to Calgary, but found it anything but easy.

"I found it really hard to see my friends and family," he says. "Mom was dead set against me going back to Swift Current. From her perspective, she had just about lost her oldest son, so she continually asked, 'Why would you want to go back?'"

Which, from a mother's perspective, seems like a reasonable question.

Her son's response was, "I have to ... for them and for me." Wilkie felt he was close to his goal of playing in the NHL, and he wasn't about to stop at this particular point in time. "I have to continue on," he told his mother.

But before he could do that, there was a memorial service and funerals.

Three of the players who died in the accident were from Saskatchewan and one was from Alberta. Chris Mantyka's funeral was in Saskatoon, Trent Kresse's in Kindersley, and Scott Kruger's in Swift Current. Brent Ruff was from Warburg, Alberta, which is where his funeral would be held.

Management split up the Broncos players to ensure that there were players at each of the funerals.

Tracy Egeland, the second-youngest player on the Broncos, had grown up on the family farm near Lethbridge. During his minor hockey career he had been coached by Randy Ruff, older brother of Lindy Ruff, the long-time head coach of the NHL's Buffalo Sabres. Brent Ruff, Randy and Lindy's younger brother, sometimes visited Lethbridge, which allowed him and Egeland to become friends. When they found themselves teammates on the Broncos, it was inevitable that the two sixteen-year-olds would become the best of friends.

"From day one," Egeland told the *Buffalo News*, "we really hit it off. It wasn't too often we were apart. Without a bus accident, I'd be talking to Brent quite a bit today regardless of where our careers and lives had taken us.

"We were going to develop into something where we would push each other and just know we had a friend to rely on no matter what. You don't meet too many people in hockey you stay friends with, because you always go from city to city. But I know Brent would have been one constant friend I always would have had."

Instead of living out those dreams, Egeland was in Warburg, a pallbearer for his best friend's funeral.

Meanwhile, Wilkie attended Scott Kruger's funeral in Swift Current.

"It was one of the saddest things I have ever been a part of," he recalls. "The church was packed and many people, including me, were sobbing uncontrollably. Scotty had been my little buddy."

Wilkie was not yet eighteen years of age. He had survived the bus accident and now he was going to view a friend in an open casket. It wasn't easy. And when he looked into the casket, he didn't see his pal.

"It wasn't the Scotty Kruger I remembered," Wilkie says. "His hair was a different colour – it was pale, kind of rose-coloured. He was all made up, not natural-looking, and he was in a suit and tie. He certainly wasn't dressed the way he usually dressed."

Scott Kruger was a little man playing a big man's game. There was no getting around it — he was only five-foot-four and 135 pounds. But, as they say, he played a lot larger than that and, naturally, he was a fan favourite.

A local boy, Kruger had put up 148 points, including 111 assists, for the junior A Swift Current Indians in 1984–85. In 1985–86, he totalled 106 points, eighty of them assists, with the Prince Albert Raiders, who dealt him to the Broncos. With his effervescent personality, Kruger quickly became a favourite among his teammates. Wilkie says Kruger was always smiling; he had one of those smiles that often resembled a smirk.

Referring to Kruger's mother Louise by her nickname, a chuckling Wilkie says, "I remember Fanner always telling him she would 'smack that smirk off your face' if he didn't stop."

Remember that this was in an era when the game of hockey was all about size, and smallish players in the NHL — and the WHL, for that matter — were few and far between. It was no secret that NHL scouts tended to look for bigger players; it was the same with the WHL, which really is a mirror image of the NHL.

Kruger knew full well that the odds were against him. That's why he would do almost anything to cut those odds down by a bit. For example, early each season, when NHL Central Scouting would send one of its scouts to visit each WHL team in order to weigh and measure individual players, Kruger would put pucks in his shorts — anything to add a few ounces to his weight. He would also put pucks in the bottom of his socks to look taller.

"He had the heart of a lion and skills that were second to none," Wilkie says.

A lot had happened in the days before Kruger's funeral, which was just another shock to Wilkie's system. After the funeral, Wilkie left the church, climbed into his car, and discovered he had no place to go. So he drove around aimlessly until, for some reason he can't explain, he found himself at the accident site.

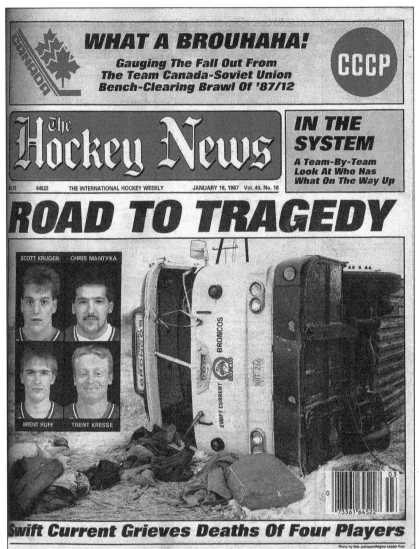

"I pulled over and just stared at the torn-up ground and cried," he says. "I was shouting, 'Why? Why God? Why?' I was not in a good place, and remember feeling darkness, emptiness … soulless."

Next was the memorial service. It was held on Sunday, January 4, with at least thirty-five hundred people filling the Centennial Civic Centre. The north and south parking lots were packed with a number of buses; each of the WHL's Eastern Division's other seven teams was in attendance. Inside, the ice surface had been covered with plywood, and a huge stage was set up on the west end of the ice. The stage held flowers, a microphone, and a table on which were displayed pictures of Kresse, Kruger, Mantyka, and Ruff. To the left of the table hung the Broncos jerseys of Kresse and Kruger; those of Mantyka and Ruff were hanging to the right.

Trent Kresse was well known in southern Saskatchewan as much for his ability on a baseball diamond as his hockey skills. He was described as sweet, sensitive, sentimental, and romantic.

Doris Kesslar, the mother of Trent's fiancée, Kari, said, "I knew if I could have hunted the world over for a perfect son-in-law, he was it. The most important thing in his life was Kari, more than hockey, more than anything. His life revolved around her."

On the ice, Kresse was the guy with the golden hands. A natural athlete, he had starred on Saskatchewan baseball diamonds since he was a kid. Like Kruger, Kresse had spent the previous season with the junior Indians, picking up eighty-two points, including fifty-four goals, in just thirty-nine games. That was enough to earn him an invitation to the Broncos' training camp, where he quickly made an impact. He was quick, he saw the ice well, and, obviously, he could score. The *Swift Current Sun* often referred to Kresse as the K-Man — he was the K-Man, and scoring goals was his assignment.

On the ice, Kresse and Kruger became the Broncos' version of Gretzky and Kurri or Bossy and Trottier. Soon, it was hard to imagine one without the other.

"They had a bond that no one else had," Wilkie says.

Kresse also made an impact on one of the Broncos' youngest players. When Tracy Egeland and his wife, Tara, welcomed a bouncing baby boy into the world in 2008, they named him Trent. The Egelands wanted to maintain the *T* theme in the family, and the name Trent just jumped out at them. Egeland says it had something to do with the fact he has fond memories of former teammate Trent Kresse.

"He was just one of the really nice guys on the team," Egeland says of Kresse, who, he adds, always treated him with respect and the utmost kindness.

———

Despite playing in the tough-as-nails WHL, Chris Mantyka, whose nickname was Chief, was remembered as a warm and kind-hearted individual. He was from Saskatoon, and while in Swift Current he lived with Broncos president John Rittinger, who said, "Mantyka was so timid he almost apologized for being alive. He never had a harsh word to say about anyone, even those who may have doubted his presence on the ice."

Graham James, the Broncos' general manager and head coach, added, "He was a player of tremendous, tremendous character. Every team needs that element to be successful and he provided it for us."

"He normally had a smile on his face," Wilkie says, "but it would disappear as soon as he strapped on his skates. He would fight in almost every game and he rarely lost a battle. Since we were a small, quick team, many of our rivals tried to intimidate us. But Chief got us the on-ice respect we needed, game in and game out. He loved being part of the Broncos and he understood his role. To me, it was plain to see that Chris Mantyka was truly happy being a Bronco."

In the words of Graham James, Brent Ruff was "the ghost of hockey's future. A player overflowing with potential, Brent was fast becoming a dominating player as a mere sixteen-year-old, perhaps the best in the country. In the future, he would've been a hundred-point man in this league."

Ruff had scored 125 goals in sixty games with a bantam team in Leduc, Alberta, the previous season, so there wasn't much doubt what his role would be down the road.

James also said, "He had that intelligence and tremendous Ruff character. It's totally numbing losing a player whose future seemed so bright. Brent loved to talk about his older brothers — Lindy, Marty, and Randy — and how proud he was of them and how he, too, had a dream of making it to the National Hockey League."

Known to his teammates as Ruffles, Wilkie remembers Ruff as a wise-cracking, confident sixteen-year-old forward who carried himself like a seasoned veteran. He obviously had grown up watching his older brothers — Lindy, who was playing in the NHL at the time, and Marty and Randy, both of whom played in the WHL — and had paid attention.

"He was healthy, happy, and talented," Wilkie says, noting that Ruff was so beloved by his teammates that he was treated more like a veteran than a rookie. There was a hierarchy with the seating on the bus — veterans sat at the back; rookies, coaches, and staff sat at the front. However, when it came to sixteen-year-old Brent Ruff, the veteran players made an exception.

"It didn't matter that he was a rookie ... he carried himself like a veteran and was welcomed as such," Wilkie says.

Peter Soberlak, who was acquired by the Broncos from the Kamloops Blazers with the season seventeen games old, couldn't believe that Ruff was only sixteen years of age.

"He was a rock-solid kid," Soberlak says. "He was seriously focused. He was going to be a pro ... I think, a great pro. No question. He was sixteen and he was on the number one line and on the number one power play. He was awesome."

The floor seats in front of the table at the memorial were occupied by members of all eight East Division teams: the Broncos, Brandon Wheat Kings, Calgary Wranglers, Medicine Hat Tigers, Moose Jaw Warriors, Prince Albert Raiders, Regina Pats, and Saskatoon Blades. Local minor hockey teams — including the midget Legionnaires and Saints, bantam Raiders, peewee Kings, and atom Lions — all were in attendance.

"It was at least a little awkward," Wilkie says of looking around and seeing so many players from other WHL teams. "Instead of fighting on the ice to defeat each other, we were on the ice to show our support as friends and family."

Indeed, the on-ice battles would have to wait.

Broncos president John Rittinger, the man who was more responsible than anyone else for the franchise having returned to his city, spoke during the service.

"We have all suffered a great loss," he said. "For many of us the grief could not possibly be greater even if our own blood families were involved."

Rittinger also spoke about the bond between the community and the team: "The people in Swift Current and the surrounding area love our Broncos. Why are they so popular? Is it because they are physically strong? Is it because they entertain us with such great skill? Certainly that is part of it, but there is much more. I think we see the young players and we see in the young players qualities we would all like to have. We have seen young people set a goal for themselves."

The crowd was moved to tears when Rittinger spoke of the fallen four: "We see dedication, determination, and intensity. Our departed teammates exemplified these qualities to the highest degree. Out of respect for these four players, no Swift Current Bronco will be permitted to wear Trent Kresse's sweater number 8, Scott Kruger's sweater number 9, Brent Ruff's sweater number 11, and Chris Mantyka's sweater number 22."

Mantyka had lived with Rittinger and his wife, Marguerite. Later, the licence plate on Rittinger's vehicle would read 8911–22; his wife's would be 22–1198.

Len Stein, then the mayor of Swift Current, also spoke. "This tragic loss has brought to our community solidarity and sorrow," he said. "A sorrow unbeknownst to us in the past, December 30, 1986, has taken from family, from friends, and from this community four young men just at the prime of their lives. This tragedy and the loss of life shall never be explainable. We shall mourn, but with the passing of time we shall go forward in dedication ever remembering Scott, Trent, Chris, and Brent."

Mayor Stein also said, "Just as the echo of their voices [is] hardly silent, we will remember [how] they gave of themselves in this very arena playing the sport they so well loved. Now, my friends, we have only our memory to hold onto. Through the founding of their memorial, Kresse, Kruger, Mantyka, and Ruff — these names and their memories shall live on. The players of today and those of tomorrow shall ever be reminded that in this great loss a provision was made. In their memory, there will be rewards. To the players of the Western Hockey League and especially to the Bronco teammates, I can only say for those who are gone, you must play on."

When WHL president Ed Chynoweth addressed the crowd, he offered the following: "For twenty years, teams in the WHL have travelled across Western Canada and the United States. Millions of miles have been logged by players and management during this time, and the majority of those miles have been by bus. Why this tragic accident occurred at this particular time we cannot answer. Why, with twenty-seven people on the bus, these particular four individuals are no longer with us, again we cannot answer. These young men were doing something they loved and dreamed of, in their apprenticeship of climbing the hockey ladder to what they hoped would be their future. Their strength of performance must now become our strength in preserving their memory and comforting their loved ones during these difficult times. Let us mark them as triumphant in their brief stay with us so their place will be on the top shelf and their minds will rest in peace."

Graham James took the podium next. He reflected on all four players, and ended his address by saying, "We've been known as a comeback team this year, and we'll come back. This is our toughest challenge."

Kurt Lackten, the team's nineteen-year-old captain, stood at the podium and, with courage belying his age, told the crowd that "the team has decided to continue the season, as I'm sure the boys would have liked."

Lackten certainly hadn't signed on for this when he stepped in as captain. His voice cracked and there were tears when he said, "We are going to miss them very much."

A story in the *Swift Current Sun* of Monday, January 5, 1987, made reference to a Canadian Press article that summarized world leaders and other prominent people who had died during 1986. "The world won't hear about Trent Kresse, Scott Kruger, Brent Ruff, and Chris Mantyka," the *Sun*'s story read, "but our community will always list them along with the famous who will be remembered in the years ahead."

The Broncos' coaching staff ended the memorial service with a message aimed at the other WHL teams in the crowd. "The message," Wilkie remembers, "was that once we were back on the ice, once we were back competing, we didn't want to be treated any differently."

The other teams were urged to "play hard, compete hard, don't back off."

James further expanded on the team's future, stating, "The toughest times may be the weeks ahead. When the schedule begins again and the publicity goes away, depression may start to appear. Alone at home at night, without family and friends, it may be hard for some of us. I don't know if something like this builds character, but it certainly reveals it. You can't say to the players, 'Go out and win it for the Gipper,' because if they lose, they may feel as though they didn't try hard enough. Everybody has aged a few years in the past few days. I think we've all got a different perspective on life now."

Rittinger echoed James's comments about the future, eloquently stating, "Anybody knows that the game of hockey is fifty percent skill, and the rest is determination and intensity. That's what we need if we're going to win. A key to our success also comes from the fan support at a time like this. Whether we win or lose should have no effect on the support. We are going to survive. We're all still stunned, but I've been here fifty years and I know this community is probably the closest-knit in the country. We'll pull through."

The day before the memorial service, the Broncos had gathered in their dressing room. James addressed the players, telling them that, considering what they had been through, any of them were free to leave the team, no questions asked.

"At that point," Wilkie says, "I don't think any of us had even thought about not playing."

Still, the players were well aware that everything was happening so fast. They also knew that decisions like these had never had to be made before, at least not on any teams on which they had played.

In the end, the players decided that, as Wilkie puts it, "every one of our dead teammates would have played on; they would have had the strength to continue."

The Broncos, then, would play again.

"But," Wilkie admits, "we knew it wasn't going to be easy."

CHAPTER 10

The Captain

On this particular Saturday, Kurt Lackten is awakened by an incoming call on his cellphone.

He is in a hotel room in Seattle. It's early afternoon. He arrived from Honolulu about 7:30 a.m. in a Boeing 767. No he wasn't a tourist; he was flying it. Lackten, the captain of the 1986–87 Swift Current Broncos, is employed by Hawaiian Airlines as a pilot.

Lackten and his wife, Julie, live in the Phoenix area, although Kurt is based in Honolulu. "I do a little bit of commuting," he says. He flies a number of routes for Hawaiian Airlines; Honolulu to Seattle is just one of them.

It wasn't supposed to turn out this way. Lackten was going to pilot hockey teams from behind the bench. But, as sometimes happens, fate threw him a curve.

As a hockey player, the native of Kamsack, Saskatchewan, was a heart-and-soul guy; a banger who wasn't a fighter, but would drop the gloves when he felt it was necessary. He prided himself on his conditioning; he was, in the vernacular, "ripped." He was selected by the New York Islanders in the seventh round, 139th overall, of the 1985 NHL draft. That came after a season in which he put up thirty-one points and 141 penalty minutes with the Moose Jaw Warriors.

During the 1985–86 season, the Warriors traded him to Medicine Hat, and twenty-seven games later, the Tigers moved him along to the Calgary Wranglers. Following the season, the Wranglers dealt him to Swift Current.

"He was a great captain, a great leader," former Broncos teammate Peter Soberlak says. "He was mature. He was composed. He had a good presence as a leader. He had a good personality ... a presence."

Lackten never did get to the NHL, playing in the American and International leagues, as well as with the East Coast leagues, before ending up in the Netherlands. It was there, with the Den Haag Wolves, that he got his first taste of coaching as a player-coach.

In the early 1990s he returned to Saskatchewan, where he spent a year attending the University of Saskatchewan in Saskatoon and playing senior hockey in the Wild Goose league. But in early 1993 he got a phone call that took him back to the Wolves.

"I went as player-coach," Lackten recalls. "I was playing, then would get back on the bench and bark out orders, and everyone would look at me like, *What the hell is he talking about?*

"So then we got a translator," he continues, and now he's chuckling. "This was the Netherlands: they speak good English, except, for some weird reason, during games they didn't want to."

Lackten, who wasn't married at the time, laughs as he remembers his European adventure. "It was a paid vacation, that's what it was," he adds. "It was fun. I met a lot of good people there, made some good friends. The schedule was super easy. Three practices a week; play on weekends. I would jump on a train on a day off, be in another country in a couple of hours. I toured around and I enjoyed that."

He also caught the coaching bug and decided that would be his life's work. So he came back to North America and caught on with the Broncos as an assistant coach. Two seasons later, he was an assistant coach in Medicine Hat.

When the Tigers made a midseason coaching change in 1997–98, Lackten found himself as the head coach. By the next season, however, he was an assistant coach with the Red Deer Rebels. He didn't know it at the time, but that was to be the last chapter in his coaching career, a move that was dictated by happenings in Toronto.

Terry Simpson, a legend in Western Canada coaching circles, had made the Prince Albert Raiders into a junior A powerhouse and was instrumental in bringing the franchise into the WHL in 1982. He was the general manager and head coach when the Raiders won the 1985 Memorial Cup. All told, he spent fifteen years coaching the Raiders.

Simpson went on to coach professionally and, by 1997–98, was an assistant coach with the Toronto Maple Leafs. Earlier, in 1992, Simpson and his brother, Wayne, had purchased a WHL expansion franchise for Red Deer. And so it was that when the Maple Leafs made some changes, Simpson chose to return to Red Deer and coach the Rebels. Which meant that head coach Doug Hobson and Lackten, his assistant coach, didn't get their contracts renewed.

"So," Lackten says, "I didn't have anything to do."

His unemployment also came at a time when there was little movement among the WHL coaching ranks. That meant that Lackten had to look at other options.

"I thought I would stay in coaching for a while," he says, "but that one year off in Red Deer when no one was hiring ... it was kind of a strange year. It gave me some time to look at things and pursue other things.

"I decided there had to be something else to do ... I looked at a whole bunch of different things and thought flying would be pretty cool, so I pursued that."

Kurt Lackten had arrived back in Swift Current on December 30, 1986, in time to get on the team bus and head to Regina for that night's game with the Pats.

"It was right after Christmas. I had just got back from driving," says Lackten, who had spent Christmas in Kamsack, a community of seventeen hundred people located about five hundred kilometres northeast of Swift Current. Darcy Hordichuk, an NHL enforcer, is from Kamsack. So is Tyler Wright, who played for the Broncos before being selected twelfth overall by the Edmonton Oilers in the NHL's 1991 draft. And so is Harold Phillipoff, who played in the WHL for Ernie McLean's big, bad New Westminster Bruins.

"I was thinking, *Great. I can go on the bus and have a little snooze and then go play,*" Lackten recalls. "And then everything happened...."

Lackten was seated by himself — he was the team captain, after all — about halfway down the left side of the bus.

"I was just dozing off and the next thing I remember ... I remember kind of waking up and there were seats everywhere. I know I was bleeding and my side hurt a lot." He was bleeding profusely from a four-inch gash on the top of his head, and found out that he had a couple of broken ribs.

Others who were on the bus tell of Lackten ignoring his injuries in order to help others.

"He was very mature.... Most of the guys were stupid kids getting in trouble," Peter Soberlak says. "Kurt was more mature. He was a leader and a captain and he acted like that, right through the bus accident. He was out there running around, taking a leadership role and helping out."

Lackten, however, says he has no memory of that. It isn't that he hasn't tried to remember, it's just that that part of his memory bank is mostly empty.

"There have been lots of times," he explains, "when I've tried to think about things and it's almost like ... I don't know how to describe it ... almost like a dream you're trying to recall but you can't. I guess that's what shock is, I don't know. Plus, I had a pretty good bonk on the head.

"I remember ... getting up and there was a seat and someone was throwing or moving a seat around. I just started walking toward the front." When asked if he helped people get off the bus or provided aid outside, Lackten responds, "I really can't say. I really don't remember helping people out. I know I went through the front, as well. Shock ... I don't really remember a whole bunch.

"I do remember walking on the highway side ... around the bus and around ... I remember doing that. And then I remember being in a van." The van took him to Swift Current Union Hospital.

What Lackten remembers more than anything else is the memorial service that was held in what was then known as the Swift Current

Centennial Civic Centre. It was January 4, 1987, and Lackten knew that, as team captain, he would have to stand up in front of the crowd — it later was estimated to be larger than 3,500 — and say … something.

He was nineteen years of age. He had survived a horrible accident in which four of his buddies had been killed. And now this kid from Kamsack was going to have to grow beyond his years, get up in front of hundreds of people, and say something.

So much had happened in such a short period of time that Lackten admits his head was spinning.

"That's maybe part of why you don't remember a whole bunch of stuff," he says now. "There was a whole bunch going on, a whole bunch to deal with."

No one on that team had been through anything like this. And, as Lackten puts it, "It wasn't like you were breaking up with your girlfriend; it wasn't that kind of emotion. This was pretty serious stuff."

So … what to say?

"I don't think there was any preparation, really," Lackten says. "I was the captain of the team; I was speaking on behalf of the team. It wasn't Kurt Lackten up there. I was just a representative … you know what I mean. There was really no preparation."

When Lackten got up in front of the crowd, he looked down and saw all of the other hockey players out there. All eight of the WHL's East Division teams were there, and teams from Swift Current minor hockey ranks were there.

Lackten spoke from his heart. Tears rolled down his cheeks as he told the crowd that the Broncos would continue their season.

He does remember the team meeting at which Graham James asked each player if he wanted to continue playing. James told the players that if any of them wanted to leave the team, there would be no repercussions; that everyone would understand.

"Looking back at that," Lackten says, "that was some pretty heavy stuff. Young players, young guys … I think everybody wanted to play. That was our goal, to be hockey players. In that situation, I think ninety-nine percent of the guys would say they wanted to continue to play. Not only the guys who were there, but if other guys were in the same situation they'd want to play."

Today, when Lackten looks back at January 4, 1987, he says, without hesitation, "That's the hardest thing I've ever had to do in my life. Bar none." That day, and his role in the memorial service, set the bar for the rest of his life. "I use that, and I've used that, throughout my life as kind of a bar. Nothing I've ever had to do has been as hard as that," he says. "I use that when I come across something that is difficult. I tell myself this isn't that bad. You know what I mean? I learned a lot of life lessons from that. I appreciate things.

"You know, when you're young you don't really … you think you've got the world by the tail and everything like that. As you get older, you come to appreciate things more and more. At that moment, there was a bitter lesson of how quickly things can get taken away from you. For me, I really appreciate things that come my way and that I have been able to accomplish … and the chances I get. Without sounding soft or mushy, it really hits home. It has had a big effect on my life and how I make decisions."

When the Broncos did get back to playing, it was in Moose Jaw against the Warriors. It was ten days after the crash. This was Swift Current's first game since before Christmas, and a lot had transpired since then. The players, Lackten included, didn't know how they would respond.

"That was pretty emotional for us," Lackten recalls. "I think the guys helped each other out a lot and obviously got a lot closer, too."

In the end, it was that closeness that got Lackten and his teammates through the most difficult season of their young lives. That first game back was even more emotional for Lackten because his WHL career had begun with the Warriors in the autumn of 1984. He still had friends, like future NHLers Theoren Fleury and Mike Keane, on the Moose Jaw roster. It meant something to have friendly faces on the ice with him in that first game, even if they now were on the opposing team.

"I had a lot of friends on the team," Lackten says. "I had a nice feeling of support there as well. Guys like Keaner coming up — and Theoren and Kevin Herom and Troy Edwards and guys like that — that was pretty important to me and a really nice thing, too."

Lackten didn't want any sympathy from those guys once the game started, nor did any of the other Broncos. But with what Lackten had been through, it was reassuring just to see some familiar faces.

———

Lackten has had a lot of time to think about what happened that blustery afternoon on a highway east of Swift Current. A lot of the memories just won't return.

"It was a long time ago," he says. "I try to remember stuff and I just can't do it."

Perhaps Lackten is a prime example of someone who has repressed memories, which, according to theory, is how some people deal with memories that are just too painful. He doesn't know if that's the case, but is of the opinion that the shock of what he went through during the first few weeks of 1987 had something to do with it. No matter; he no longer tries to figure it out. He does know that he learned quite a life lesson the day the bus crashed and in the days and nights that followed.

"A hockey game is sixty minutes," he says. "It's like a life. It's got its peaks, its valleys ... its highs, its lows. It's life. It's all right there. Sixty minutes: there's a whole life, you know what I mean?

"I think being in sports, you learn that you can't really dwell on things because it's going to affect the next thing that you have to deal with. So you do move on, especially if there's nothing that you can affect or change.

"But I'm not a psychologist ... I'm just a pilot."

CHAPTER 11

The Trainer

Gord Hahn wasn't even on the Swift Current Broncos' bus on the night of December 30, 1986, but he has never been able to shake what happened.

Hahn, the Broncos' trainer, and defenceman Dan Lambert were with Team Western, an under-seventeen team that was playing exhibition games against a touring Russian squad in venues across the Prairies. In fact, it was Lambert who broke the news to Hahn, who has long been known by his nickname — he spells it Hahnda.

"I was in Winnipeg at the time with Team Western, me and Danny Lambert," recalls Hahn, who still lives in Swift Current and is semi-retired. "I heard about it during the first period. Danny called me over and said, 'We gotta go in the dressing room, I lost a contact.' We went in the dressing room and he just broke down. I said, 'Geez, Danny, what's the matter? What's going on?'

"Then he told me what happened. He knew. They weren't supposed to tell me until after the game. The coaches told him. They didn't tell me because they knew I would just lose it."

Hahn, the veteran trainer, and Lambert, the sixteen-year-old WHL rookie, spent the remainder of the first period in the dressing room.

"I couldn't go back on the bench for the rest of the period," Hahn says. "I was ... *This can't be happening.* We both sat in there for the rest of the period."

Hahn was a long-time junior hockey trainer. He had been with the Brandon Wheat Kings in the early 1970s and also had a stint with the Victoria Cougars before moving to Swift Current and working with Pat Ginnell's junior A Indians. Hahn knew his way around just about every junior hockey arena in western Canada and some in the United States. In the end, he wouldn't be a junior hockey lifer, but at the time of the bus accident he certainly appeared to be headed in that direction.

In 1984–85, when Regina's WHL franchise had almost been sold to interests in Swift Current, the Pats were coached by Bill Moores, a long-time University of Alberta Golden Bears head coach who would go on to a lengthy career as an NHL assistant coach, and Bill Liskowich, a veteran of the Saskatchewan coaching wars. As it turned out, Liskowich, a highly compassionate man, was on the Team Western coaching staff.

"Bill Liskowich is a super guy," says Hahn, who was thirty-nine years of age on December 30, 1986. "He came into the dressing room and talked to us and got us settled down. He said, 'If you want to go home we'll fly you home right now. There's a ticket at the airport.' I said, 'No, we'll stick it out. We're here for a reason so let's get on with it.'"

You have to understand the relationship between a trainer — today, they more often are called athletic therapists — and his or her players. Perhaps that relationship is best likened to the bond between a mother cat and her kittens. Often the trainer has been around for a while and has seen most everything; the players, meanwhile, are away from home, some of them for the first time, and may have few, if any, confidants. The trainer, then, does it all, from tending to injuries to offering guidance and taking confession.

And here was Hahn in an arena in Winnipeg, wondering what had happened to his team — his boys — some 815 kilometres to the west.

After the game in Winnipeg, Team Western boarded a bus and headed for Athol Murray College of Notre Dame, which is located just south of Regina in Wilcox. The team would bunk there before playing the Russians in Saskatoon.

"That was a painful ride ... something I'll never forget," Hahn recalls. "We drove through a couple of storms that night, too. I kept my eye on the bus driver. I told him, 'If you don't want to drive, don't drive.' He was just shaking all the way [to Wilcox]."

Team Western, including Hahn and Lambert, went on to play that game in Saskatoon, after which it again returned to Notre Dame. By then, Hahn was in a state of near frenzy. He wanted so badly to be with the players who meant so much to him.

"I got everything put away and the players settled in," he says. It was well after midnight. "I hopped in my car to come home because I wanted to be home to get ready for the memorial service and stuff like that."

As he approached Swift Current and the site of the bus accident, he fell asleep at the wheel of his car.

He tells the story as if it happened yesterday: "I was driving right by the bridge ... I was in the westbound lane. I woke up on the shoulder ... I was doing maybe twenty or thirty [kilometres per hour] because I let off the gas when I fell asleep.

"All of a sudden, I was there where it happened. I went, 'Oh my God, this is it.' That shook the cobwebs out. I got home and couldn't sleep. I hadn't slept for four days — unbelievable — because everything was going through my head."

These days, Hahn says he stops and visits the accident site almost every time he drives past it.

"When I drive by that spot," he explains, "I go right down and look up and, you know, say something to myself. It's tough."

(In fact, Hahn has worked for some time trying to get a sign in the shape of a four-leaf clover erected at the site. "The Department of Highways has a policy," he says, "but you see crosses on the side of the road where accidents happen. They're more concerned about a sign ... if somebody sees it they might run off the road or whatever. I'm still working on it.")

Hahn had been especially close to Chris Mantyka, the rough-and-ready winger from Saskatoon. Mantyka had first arrived in Swift Current to play with the junior A Indians, the team for which Hahn worked as trainer.

"When the Broncos came back that year, I actually asked if he could try out at training camp," Hahn says. "They weren't thinking about having him in camp. I said, 'Just give him a try. He's tougher than nails and you won't find a nicer kid.' He was so mature. So they gave him a try and they really liked him ... and that happened."

"That" has haunted Hahn since it happened. What if he hadn't asked the Broncos to take Mantyka to training camp? "That haunts me … it's never-ending," Hahn says.

Before the bus accident, Hahn had never had problems sleeping. And Hahn wasn't on the bus when it crashed. "Now I can't sleep in a car, I can't sleep in a bus … anything. It just totally hooped me," Hahn says, a tremor in his voice.

"All four of them … I was really close to them."

Hahn remembers a team meeting called by Graham James. Assistant coach Lorne Frey says it was held the afternoon of January 3, 1987, the day before the memorial service. The team gathered in its dressing room.

"Graham went around to each guy individually," Hahn says, "and asked, 'Would you like to continue the season or would you like to pack it in? It's your choice and I'll back you up either way.' He went to each guy individually, including myself, and we said, 'No, we want to keep going.'"

Frey concurs. "Whether we continued playing … I don't think that was ever an issue," Frey says. "He gave some of the players the option: 'Whether you want to continue or whether you don't want to continue, that would be your choice. If this was too much for you and you want to go home, you can go home.'" It was, Frey says, a choice offered to each player as an individual. No one who was at that meeting left the team.

After the meeting, the team headed to a local pizza joint, and that's when what had transpired over the last while hit Hahn like a ton of bricks. "We went out for a pizza night at one of the pizza places and that's when I really got close with the players," Hahn says, the memory of the night as bright as a full moon. "It was like — *holy!* I couldn't stop shaking. It was unbelievable." It was then when Hahn decided that something had to be done so that the memories of the four deceased players would live forever.

Later, Hahn happened to be on the phone with Norm Fong, a long-time friend who was the veteran equipment manager for the CFL's Saskatchewan Roughriders. That conversation was the genesis of the four-leaf clover that now adorns the Broncos' jerseys.

After talking it over with Fong, Hahn called a company in Winnipeg and two days later had a package in his hands that included four-leaf clover patches that would be sewn onto the jerseys before the Broncos played their next game. While the patch has since been redesigned, with each petal displaying one of the fallen players' sweater numbers, it continues to pay tribute on the right shoulder of every one of the Broncos jerseys.

By 1988–89, Hahn was working for the city of Swift Current and volunteering with the Broncos, who won the WHL championship and advanced to the Memorial Cup tournament, which would be held in Saskatoon. Hahn wasn't able to get time off work in order to spend a week in Saskatoon, so he drove back and forth in order to work the Broncos' games.

"I did all the equipment stuff that season, skate sharpening, repairs, all that stuff," he recalls. And he was on the Broncos' bench when Tim Tisdale scored the overtime goal that gave the Broncos a 4–3 victory over the host Blades in the four-team tournament's championship final.

"Was it ever emotional! I broke down after the goal," Hahn says. "They were out on the ice celebrating. I stayed by the dressing room … I broke down just thinking about the four guys." Later, the Broncos would get Memorial Cup championship rings. "I was pumped when they made the rings and put the four-leaf clover on them," Hahn says.

These days, when he looks back at his days with the Broncos, his eyes mist over and there is a catch in his voice.

"It was an honour being a part of the Swift Current organization," he says, "and working with a lot of great hockey players. We went through a lot together."

Dan Lambert was known to his teammates as 'Pepe' because he is from the French-speaking community of St. Malo, Manitoba.

"Danny had a great sense of humour and could easily make the team laugh at any time," Bob Wilkie says. "Pepe was another character who was fun to watch as a young defenceman because he could rush the puck from end to end, he was physical and he would fight anybody, and he was a huge asset to the team."

Lambert would go on to be named the most valuable player of the 1989 Memorial Cup in Saskatoon, where he put up eight points in five games. That included two assists in the Broncos' 5–4 overtime victory over the host Blades in the championship game.

Rod Steensland.

Danny Lambert (3) was a puck-moving defenceman who wasn't afraid to venture deep into the other team's zone.

"When we came back in [to the dressing room], I just sat in my stall and thought things over," Lambert told Ed Willes of the *Regina Leader-Post*. "You see it on TV and you dream about it, but you never expect something like this to happen. Today it happened for me."

Lambert, who played in twenty-nine NHL games with the Quebec Nordiques before going on to a lengthy career in Germany, now is an assistant coach with the Kelowna Rockets.

"Life has been very good to me," Lambert says. "Hockey has given me everything ... the experiences of living all over the world. It's been great and I don't want it to end, which might explain why I'm still [involved with] this great game. I am pursuing a coaching career and hope to give back to the game because it has given my family and I so much."

CHAPTER 12

The Uncle

Lorne Frey is currently the assistant general manager, head scout, and director of player personnel with the WHL's Kelowna Rockets. In 1986, however, he was the Swift Current Broncos' assistant coach. Louise "Fanner" Kruger was his sister, meaning Frey had two nephews on the bus that crashed, one of whom didn't survive.

At the hospital following the accident, it was Frey who informed Louise and her husband, Walt (Scoof), that four players, including their son Scott, had died.

As is standard when junior hockey teams travel by bus, the coaching staff sits up front. That's where Frey was as the Broncos turned onto the Trans-Canada Highway and headed east to Regina for a game on the night of December 30, 1986.

"We came over the bridge," Frey remembers. "It was windy and icy and the bus started fishtailing and we drove into the ditch. Everyone was yelling, 'Hold on! Hold on!'"

There is no bitterness in Frey's voice as he remembers that ugly afternoon, but he does wonder what might have happened had driver Dave Archibald done one thing differently.

"You can second-guess everything but had [Archibald] gone straight out into the pasture, we'd have been fine," Frey explains. "But he pulled it back up on the road and it came back down.... You didn't think anything of it and then everybody's yelling, 'Hang on! Hang on!' The killer was hitting the approach."

At the time, Frey says, "We didn't think anything of it." In other words, no one had any idea of the carnage that would follow.

With the bus in obvious difficulty, Frey got out of his seat — he was on the left side, three rows behind the driver — and stood in the aisle. "I grabbed onto the seats," Frey says. "I figured if we were going to roll, I'm not going to get caught rolling around in my seat. So I stood up in the aisle and grabbed the seats. I remember us taking off and I remember the back coming down. Then the bus rolled on its side ... everybody's yelling, and then it was over ... and I didn't think, *Everybody okay?* and then the four kids...."

Three of the players — Trent Kresse, Scott Kruger, and Brent Ruff — suffered broken necks. "Those guys were in the back," Frey remembers. "The bus went airborne and then the back wheels came down and shot them up [into the roof] and that's where they broke their necks."

All four of the players who died ended up outside the bus, two of them well clear and two underneath — something Frey can't understand.

"I don't know how those guys got out of the bus. I have no idea to this day how they got out of that bus," he says. "The windows at the back were this big." He holds his hands out to form a small circle. "There were four [players] outside. I have no idea how they got out there."

Frey wasn't injured. No cuts, not even a bruise, he says. "I was fine. The bus rolled and I was just leaning against the seats."

Once the bus quit sliding, Frey, along with everyone else, scrambled out the front, where the windshield used to be. "It was totally quiet. The bus rolled and slid — I don't know how far — and nobody said anything then," Frey says. "Then after it stopped everyone was saying, 'Okay, everybody all right, everybody okay, everybody all right.' We had no idea what was going on outside. We had no idea what was happening outside ... that those kids were outside.

"I went out and I couldn't believe those guys were outside the bus. Our trainer, Doug Leavins, was looking at those kids and there was nothing there," Frey says, and there is anguish in his eyes.

While Frey lost a nephew in the accident, he also lost Chris Mantyka, who he says was "one of my favourites." He remembers Mantyka, who had spent 1985–86 with the junior A Swift Current Indians, coming into the Broncos' office over the summer.

"He comes in … he's this big hulking kid who played junior A there the year before," Frey says with a chuckle. "He says to me, his head's down, 'Lorne, can I try out this year?' I said, 'Absolutely.' We kept him, and after that every time I came in the room he'd give me a big hug and it'd be, 'Gee it's great, thanks for keeping me.' He was just a great kid.

"We'd practise and get him working with the younger guys because the older guys were on the power play and stuff. The younger guys were afraid of him. I'd say, 'Chris, Chris, you gotta lay off these guys a little bit. Just relax.' He'd come back with, 'But, Lorne, I've gotta get better, too.' 'Yeah,' I'd say, 'but you don't have to beat them up.'"

Frey says Mantyka played the game for keeps and he didn't pick his spots, not even in practice. Frey remembers Mantyka fighting Ian Herbers, a towering defenceman, in one practice, and going with team captain Kurt Lackten in another. After the fight with Lackten, Frey says, Graham James wanted to get rid of Mantyka. Frey talked James out of that, and a month into the season, a laughing Frey says, Mantyka was one of James's favourites, too.

Frey has been around the WHL for a long time. He has taken many bus trips since the accident, but it wasn't until early in the 2010–11 season that he was able to put his head back, close his eyes, and actually sleep.

"Lornie has had a tough time of it," says Bruce Hamilton, the president and general manager of the Rockets. "But I finally saw him sleeping on the bus when we were coming back from a game in Vancouver." That was after an exhibition game prior to the 2010–11 season, almost twenty-four years after the accident.

Frey is quite content to work like most scouts: in the background, well away from the glare of the spotlight. During the run to the 1989 Memorial Cup and in the media glow afterward, it was Graham James who got a lot of the attention.

In a brief conversation in April 2009, James talked about how Frey was such an integral part of the Broncos.

Darren Kruger with wife, Beverly, and daughter, Emily.

"Lorne … was much underappreciated for the players he contributed to the team. The Krugers and Tisdale … a lot of guys he stuck with," James said. For example, the Broncos already had a smallish defenceman in Danny Lambert, who was a brilliant puck-mover. So did they really have room on the roster for another defenceman from the same mould?

"Darren Kruger was unbelievable," James said. "We had Lambert and I'm thinking, *Can we afford another guy who is five-foot-six on the*

Rod Steensland.

Leesa Culp and Lorne Frey at the 2009 Swift Current Broncos Hall of Fame induction dinner honouring the 1989 Memorial Cup–winning team

team? Lorne pushed me and pushed me on Kruger. He turned out to be a huge difference-maker for the Broncos and one of the best guys I ever coached. And the same with Trevor."

Like Frey, Trevor Kruger doesn't get nearly the credit he should for the success the Broncos had in 1988–89. Remember that this was in the days before hockey's deep thinkers decided to put trapezoids behind the goals and restrict goaltenders to handling the puck only in that area. Back in the day, teams that played a quick transition game needed a puck-handling goaltender. Kruger was just that for the Broncos. He would pick up a dumped-in puck and get it to one of his defencemen quicker than you could blink. It was only a coincidence that the Krugers were also Frey's nephews.

"Lornie Frey, I've known him since the days he was working with Jackie McLeod in Saskatoon, and he's still finding players," James said. "That's a helluva career."

One of the keys to Frey's success, according to James, is that he is his own man. "Lorne never played the political game, never kissed anybody's ass to get ahead," James said. "He is just who he is and who he is is very good. He was never a guy who wanted to play that game. And he never will. He could scout for any pro team."

After winning the 1989 Memorial Cup, the Broncos would win the WHL's 1992–93 championship. By then, Frey was with the Tacoma Rockets, the predecessor to the Kelowna Rockets, as alternate governor, assistant general manager, and director of player personnel. Bruce Franklin, now a scout with the NHL's Chicago Blackhawks, was then the Broncos' director of player personnel.

"When I look back, we were fortunate in Swift Current," James said. "We had Lornie, who really knew the league. We had Bruce Franklin, who came in and did a good job. Then we had Paul Charles, who was outstanding. That's what it's all about."

The Broncos of that era were proof that in junior hockey, if you don't have good scouts, you don't have success.

CHAPTER 13

Just an Ordinary Joe

There isn't much doubt about who was the best player on the 1986–87 Swift Current Broncos. That would be Joe Sakic, the quiet, unassuming, soon-to-be superstar who put up 133 points as a rookie the season the bus crashed. For that, he was named the East Division's rookie of the year.

Sakic would play only one more season in Swift Current — he put up 160 points in 1987–88 — so he wasn't part of the team that won the 1989 Memorial Cup. The Quebec Nordiques selected him with the fifteenth pick of the NHL's 1987 draft. He was on his way to a sixty-two-point rookie NHL season when the Broncos were on the road to winning the Memorial Cup.

Sakic was born July 7, 1969, to Marijan and Slavica Sakic, Croatian immigrants who had settled in Burnaby, British Columbia. Growing up as the son of immigrants, Sakic developed a strong work ethic, and it was that, along with an abundance of skill, more on-ice patience than any player should have, and an ability to see the ice and read the play, that helped him carve out quite a niche in the NHL.

"We never had it easy growing up," Sakic told Larry Wigge of *The Sporting News* for a January 2002 story. "Dad worked for everything we had. He never let me off the hook. In hockey it was the same thing: 'Get out there and work.'

"Even today, after a bad game, there are times when I won't answer the phone. I know who it is. Even though I'm all grown up, I know it's my dad calling to tell me he had seen the game, and he's going to tell me I didn't work hard enough."

By the time Sakic retired after the 2008–09 season, he had recorded 1,641 points in the NHL, including 625 goals, in 1,378 regular-season games. He also was one of those rarities in today's game — a one-organization man. He had been drafted by the Nordiques and made the move to Denver over the summer of 1995 when the Quebec franchise became the Colorado Avalanche.

In fact, he played for only two organizations in his career, from major junior through his NHL days.

Sakic began his WHL career with the Lethbridge Broncos — he was pointless in three games with them in 1985–86 — and was one of the players who at first wasn't interested in moving when the franchise was sold to Swift Current interests.

But move he did, and he wound up playing a starring role in Swift Current. In his second and final season there, he finished with 160 points, including seventy-eight goals, in sixty-four games. He ended up tied atop the WHL scoring race with Theoren Fleury of the Moose Jaw Warriors, who also had 160 points. Sakic was given the scoring championship on the basis of having scored more goals than Fleury, 78–68.

Sakic rarely has spoken publicly about the bus accident. He and frequent linemate Sheldon Kennedy were seated near the front of the bus, chatting about the Christmas each had experienced. In 2002, Sakic told Wigge, "Clearly, you grow up in a hurry after something like that. It changes your whole outlook on life and makes you appreciate what you have even more. That matured us all, I think."

When interviewed by Brian Costello of *The Hockey News* for a story that appeared in the December 27, 1996, issue, Sakic said, "You never forget that day. It makes you realize that it could end at any time for anybody. Sometimes when I drive around, I think about it. It makes you careful."

Sakic told writer Debbie Elicksen, "The best thing was during practices and games — that was the best time to get away. You just focused on hockey.

Trevor Kruger (left), Peter Soberlak, Bob Wilkie, Sheldon Kennedy, Chris Larkin, and Darren Kruger get ready for a round of golf the day following the twenty-year reunion dinner for the team that won the 1989 Memorial Cup.

"It was the first time a tragedy happened in my life. Kind of reality checks in. You're a little more careful about the things you decide to do. You weigh the options, I guess."

Roy MacGregor of the *Globe and Mail* spoke with Sakic in February 2008. "It's tough," Sakic told MacGregor. "You can't believe what happened. You just don't believe it. It's tough to think about it and it's something you never forget. You want to overcome it all, but these are your friends. You can't forget. You don't want to forget. All you know for sure is that, in time, things will get better."

When writer Gare Joyce was researching a story that would appear on *www.ESPN.com*, Sakic agreed to talk to him. But, according to Joyce's story, only "on the condition that no questions would be asked about the details of the crash."

When the authors of this book requested an interview with Sakic through his agent, Don Baizley, the NHL star chose to take a pass.

"He is a class act and always has been … a future Hall of Famer, a Stanley Cup champion, and a gold-medal winner in the Olympics," former teammate Bob Wilkie says of Sakic. "He was a blast to play with and to watch and he was a huge part of the success we had over the two seasons…. He was a quiet guy who never really said much. His actions spoke louder than words."

Peter Soberlak, who was traded to the Broncos by the Kamloops Blazers early in the 1986–87 season, frequently played on a line with Sakic. Soberlak says that Joe has always been, well, Joe.

"He is absolutely a good guy," Soberlak says. "He has never changed."

Because Sakic was in the NHL when the Swift Current team won the 1989 Memorial Cup, he wasn't officially a part of the 1989 reunion celebration that was held in Swift Current in August 2009. That doesn't mean Sakic wasn't there, though. His wife, Debbie, is from Swift Current, so they and their three children are frequent visitors to the city. Whether by coincidence or good management, the Sakics were there when the 1988–89 team was holding its twentieth anniversary celebration. Part of the celebration involved a golf tournament.

"Myself, Sheldon [Kennedy], Danny [Lambert], and Wilkie were in the last foursome," Soberlak says, adding that Sakic made a non-playing appearance early in the proceedings. "He drove around with us from the third hole on…. It was like we were seventeen again. He was just Joe." It didn't matter, Soberlak says, that Sakic had made "$100 million or something like that" in his career. He was just Joe.

"Sheldon was giving it to him about his dogs and stuff," Soberlak says. "And it wasn't long before it was just, 'Ah, shut up Sakic.'

"He really was just Joe."

CHAPTER 14

The Coroner's Report

It wasn't long after the accident involving the Swift Current Broncos' bus that Swift Current coroner d'Arcy Morrice called an inquest into the tragedy. At the same time, the *Swift Current Sun* reported on January 12, 1987, that the vehicle standards and inspection department of Saskatchewan Government Insurance (SGI) was also going to investigate the accident.

By February 9, Morrice had completed his report, in which he made four recommendations:

1. Teams should allot more time for travel when weather is inclement;
2. The WHL should encourage teams to postpone or cancel road trips should weather conditions result in dangerous driving conditions;
3. Teams should use buses that feature some form of restraining devices, and should enforce the usage of such devices; and
4. The province of Saskatchewan should enact legislation requiring buses carrying teams within the province to be equipped with adequate restraining devices, and the use of these devices should be enforced.

According to Morrice's report, the Broncos' bus had been in good operating condition. No charges were ever laid.

Morrice also released the cause of death for the four deceased players. They had been seated in the back of the bus, in pairs across from each other while playing cards.

Trent Kresse, Scott Kruger, and Brent Ruff died due to dislocation of the cervical spine. They had been thrown upwards, and their heads had hit the roof of the bus. Chris Mantyka died of traumatic asphyxia — he was crushed after he somehow ended up under the bus.

Immediately following the accident, the *Swift Current Sun* printed a list of survivors. That list included twenty-four names — six adults and eighteen players. While researching this book, it was learned that one of the people whose name was on the list — goaltender Bob Crockett — had not been on the bus. Here is the list, as it appeared in the *Sun*:

Adults:
Graham James, general manager and coach
Lorne Frey, assistant coach
John Foster, public relations director
Dave Archibald, bus driver
Doug Leavins, assistant trainer
Brian Costello, *Swift Current Sun* sports writer
Players:
Ed Brost, defence, 19
Gord Green, defence, 19
Ian Herbers, defence, 19
Sheldon Kennedy, forward, 17
Tim Tisdale, forward, 18
Joe Sakic, forward, 17
Pat Nogier, goal, 18
Clarke Polglase, defence, 17
Bob Wilkie, defence, 17
Kurt Lackten, forward/captain, 19
Tracy Egeland, forward, 16

Trevor Kruger, goal, 18
Peter Soberlak, forward, 17
Lonnie Spink, forward, 19
Jason Proulx, defence, 18
Artie Feher, goal, 20
Bob Crockett, goal, 16
Todd Sceviour, forward, 19

CHAPTER 15

Back on the Ice

It was an emotionally exhausted group of Swift Current Broncos who returned to the ice following the January 4 memorial service honouring the four players who had been killed in the crash of the team's bus.

The surviving players' heads were spinning with all that had transpired since the accident on the afternoon of December 30. But they knew they had to get on with their lives.

The Broncos had missed four games, but they would make those up as the season progressed. In the meantime, their first game post-accident was scheduled for January 9 in Moose Jaw against the Warriors.

Obviously, most of the players were still nursing bumps and bruises to one degree or another. Defenceman Bob Wilkie's right hip, which originally was thought to have been broken, wasn't, but it was stiff, and his face still showed evidence of having been banged around.

Forward Kurt Lackten, the team captain, was nursing tender ribs. Peter Soberlak, another forward, had a sore shoulder. And on and on....

Meanwhile, Graham James had been busy working the phones because his roster had been left with four holes — the spots that had belonged to the players who had died in the crash.

"It's a very difficult situation where things are not clear cut," James told the *Swift Current Sun*. "You can't look in the phone book and find 'dial-a-tragedy' because nobody really has the answers.

"We're going to try and stick with the players on our list and help ourselves. I don't want to downplay the assistance of other teams, but the players offered to us would have to go back next [season] or simply be borderline players. By reaching into our own list, we can develop better as a team. And you don't want to bring strange players into a difficult situation like this, have them help you and then shake their hand goodbye two weeks later. How can you do that? How can you even cut a player who had to go through this?"

In the days immediately after the accident, the WHL developed a plan whereby each of the league's other thirteen teams would offer up one player. A list of those players would be compiled and the Broncos then would choose two or three of them.

Erin Ginnell, who had played with the junior A Swift Current Indians the previous season, and Swift Current native Garth Lamb were the chosen two. Ginnell, one of coaching legend Pat Ginnell's sons, already had played that season with the Seattle Thunderbirds and Regina Pats. Lamb had been with the Victoria Cougars.

(Erin Ginnell, today a scout for the NHL's Florida Panthers, is convinced that the Pats offered him to the Broncos fully expecting to hear, "Thanks, but no thanks." Ginnell's theory is that the Pats, knowing full well the animosity between John Rittinger and Ginnell's father — animosity that had developed while both men pursued a WHL franchise for Swift Current — expected the Broncos to turn down their offer of help. The Broncos, however, were glad to welcome the younger Ginnell aboard.)

James was also able to acquire some other help. He got left-winger Blair Atcheynum, a seventeen-year-old who had asked the Saskatoon Blades for a trade. Later, James would deal him to Moose Jaw for veteran defenceman Tim Logan.

Right-winger David Aldred, a sixteen-year-old who had been playing junior A in Grande Prairie, Alberta, was brought in and put right onto a line with Joe Sakic and Sheldon Kennedy. Another right winger, Terry Baustad, who had played in Moose Jaw and Calgary, also was added.

Wilkie says that when the Broncos regrouped, they found a different attitude in their dressing room. "Before the accident, there was a feeling that at least some of us were just glad to be in the WHL," he explains. "Now there was a new feeling taking hold that we were in this together, that we didn't want any sympathy on the ice, that we wanted to make the playoffs, and that we were determined to do just that."

While the players eagerly awaited the arrival of January 9, there also was a feeling of dread as the day approached. After all, they were going to have to get back on a bus. With the Broncos' bus having been totalled, the Saskatchewan Transportation Company provided the team with a bus for use on the trip to Moose Jaw.

"Frankly," Wilkie says, "I was scared out of my wits." Still, he kept his feelings to himself as he tried to convince himself that it was good to be back on the bus, that it was good to be heading out to play a game again, that it was good to get back into something of a routine. But deep inside he felt terrible.

"To this day," he says, "when I go over a hump in a road and get that uneasy feeling like my insides have lifted, it freaks me out."

On January 9, as the Broncos' bus drove past the accident site, Wilkie turned up his Walkman, closed his eyes, and tried to lose himself. He was listening to Bon Jovi and the tune was "Livin' on a Prayer."

You had to have been in the Moose Jaw Civic Centre that night to understand the raw emotion that was in the building. From the moment you walked into the building, you could feel it. It was as though every person in the arena was aware of just how badly this group of young men needed to feel support and affection. These men, most of them still in their teenage years, had been through a mind-numbing series of experiences over the previous ten days. They needed a hug.

"We were trying hard to make this game just like all the games that had preceded it," Wilkie recalls. "But we knew that wasn't the case. And as we got closer to the dropping of the puck, we could feel the anticipation growing. We also could feel an incredible energy from inside the building."

Courtesy of Leesa Culp.

The 3,146-seat arena in Moose Jaw, a.k.a. the Crushed Can, where the Broncos played their first game after the bus crash. The Crushed Can was replaced by Mosaic Place prior to the 2011–12 season and was demolished in the summer of 2012.

At the same time, some players weren't sure their minds or their bodies were ready for the rigours of playing again. And whether or not it was because of all they'd been through, there would be more injuries.

Sheldon Kennedy, already with a bruised right shoulder that would cost him a handful of games, would go down with a hairline fracture to an ankle in January. Soberlak, playing with a sore arm, took a whack across a calf in one of his first games back. Jason Proulx had a bad arm. (To make matters worse, Proulx didn't even want to be with the Broncos. Acquired with Soberlak from the Kamloops Blazers in a trade for forward Warren Babe, Proulx had requested a trade before Christmas. He had returned to Swift Current after Christmas hoping to be moved as soon as possible, and had been on the bus when it crashed.)

And then, in one of those early games, Lackten, who already was nursing sore ribs, went down with a concussion. Later, goaltender Pat Nogier would find himself with a sore arm, Blair Atcheynum a slightly separated shoulder, and Danny Lambert a sore hip and bruised knee.

The hits, it seemed, were just going to keep on coming.

But right now the Broncos were in Moose Jaw and — finally — the moment had arrived.

Goaltender Trevor Kruger stood up in the dressing room and led his teammates out the door and down the hallway to the ice for the pre-game skate. It was a fairly long walk, made even longer by the moment, but they got there. When they did, they were met by a wall of noise.

If you have been in the Civic Centre, you understand the makeup of the building. It wasn't called the Crushed Can for nothing. It actually had a metal roof, and it did resemble a crushed can. You might say it was a poor man's — a really poor man's — Calgary Saddledome. If you were seated midway up on one side of the building, you couldn't see the stands on the other side. That also meant there was nowhere for the noise to go — and as the Broncos stepped onto the ice, the crowd roared its appreciation.

The Broncos were sporting new sweaters, each one with a newly sewn-on four-leaf clover on the right shoulder. The Civic Centre was jam-packed with a record crowd of 3,463 cheering fans — about five hundred of them loyal supporters from Swift Current — and for two minutes they stood and cheered, showing their respect and admiration for the visiting team. While Moose Jaw regularly drew decent crowds to the Civic Centre — at that time, it was listed as having 3,030 seats and room for three hundred standees — the Crushed Can never had seen anything like this.

By this point, most of the Broncos simply were trying to keep it together. It was a battle they couldn't win, and it wasn't long before the tears began to flow.

Somehow the Broncos got through their warm-up and returned to the dressing room so the Zamboni could clean the ice.

In the Broncos' dressing room, there was silence. There wasn't any of the talking or kibitzing that usually precedes a game. When the ice was cleared, the Broncos went back out and were met by another standing ovation, this one even louder than the first.

Once the crowd quieted, there was a moment of silence as the crowd honoured the memories of the four Broncos who had died in the bus crash. And, as the crowd burst into "O Canada," the eyes of the Swift Current players were glistening.

Finally, the game was underway and, like most games, it slipped neatly into that familiar rhythm — the give and take, the back and forth, the banging and crashing, the shots, the saves.

The crowd was into this one, too. The Swift Current fans would begin a chorus of 'Go Broncos Go,' only to be greeted by 'Go Warriors Go' from the Moose Jaw fans. But it became evident early on that the Broncos weren't going to be able to put on their skates and slide right back into the routine of playing hard.

"We were going through the motions," Wilkie says, adding that "at the same time, I just couldn't believe that the Warriors were playing so hard." Wilkie admits that he caught himself feeling sorry for himself and his teammates. "Didn't they know we had been through a horrible time?" he was asking himself. Years later, he admits that he really didn't want to be in Moose Jaw that night.

"I really wanted to be somewhere else … anywhere else," he says.

In the end, the Warriors won the game 6–5, but the Broncos didn't feel like losers. Mainly, they felt relief that the first game was over.

Their next game was against the Pats in the Regina Agridome, and again they received a standing ovation from the home team's fans. It was a pattern that would be repeated in every arena they visited. Time and again the fans would rise and show their support and appreciation.

The Broncos played their first home game since the accident on January 13 against the Medicine Hat Tigers. The teams were greeted by 2,459 fans who showered the Broncos with noise, love, and appreciation. The Tigers showed no mercy.

"By now," Wilkie says, "we were spent emotionally and really, really needed a break in order to regroup." The Tigers whipped them 6–1. This was a young Swift Current team and, in truth, what it had been through since Christmas was catching up with the players.

"We were young," Wilkie says, "most of us were away from home for the first time, and we had been through a lot in a short period of time. In all honesty, we were lost. Our hearts were heavy and in a lot of ways we had no sense of direction."

Brian Costello of the *Swift Current Sun*, who had been on the bus that fateful day, had even described the players in print as "soldiers of misfortune."

In hindsight, Wilkie wonders if the players weren't suffering from some sort of post-traumatic stress disorder. After all, they had been involved in an accident that had claimed four teammates. The surviving players had only been able to go home for a day or two, if at all. No counsellors had been brought in. There had been four funerals and a memorial service. The season had resumed. All in a matter of ten days.

And now, to make matters worse, Graham James, the general manager and head coach, had become an angry, angry man.

Wilkie recalls: "He never had been shy about showing us his temper and he would rant when we weren't playing well. But it all seemed more intense after the accident. Even the next season, 1987–88, he didn't have the tantrums he had right after the accident. Maybe he seemed harsher because we were hurting so much, but it seemed brutal at times.

"He had turned into a short-tempered coach who was quick to yell at and berate his charges. He had never been one to shy away from criticizing his players, but never before had he done it with such anger in his voice and mannerisms. And now he wasn't shy about berating his own players right on the bench, which meant it would happen in front of the fans."

Wilkie says he will never forget one home game against Regina when "we got a real ass-whipping. He didn't do it on the bench — he saved it for the dressing room. He roared into the room after the game, ripped down the dressing-room stereo, and threw it against the wall. The moment the stereo bounced off the wall was the moment I lost all respect for Graham, and I know a lot of the other players felt the same way."

The Broncos ran hot and cold for the rest of that hockey season, and had it not been for Joe Sakic, who really was starting to come onto hockey's radar, the season may have been totally lost. Sakic simply was on fire for the season's second half. He would finish with 133 points, the fourth-highest total in the WHL, including sixty goals.

The Broncos also were drawing a lot of interest from NHL scouts, who were flocking to their games to watch the likes of Kennedy, Sakic, Wilkie, Soberlak, and Ryan McGill. While watching the Broncos and Medicine Hat one night, veteran scout Glen Sonmor said, "I've never been to a single game where so many potential first-round draft picks are playing."

Rod Steensland.

The Broncos – in this case, Peter Soberlak (16) and Tim Tisdale (13) – loved to apply pressure to the opposing goaltender.

In the end, the Broncos qualified for the playoffs, their 28–40–4 record good enough for the East Division's sixth and final playoff spot.

On the night they clinched a playoff spot, promotions director John Foster hung up the telephone, stuck out a hand, and delivered the news: "Congratulations, Graham, you're in the playoffs."

A chorus of whoops and yells followed: "We're in! We're in!" Players and management shouted it loudly and proudly in the dressing room. The players were jumping up and down and stomping their feet.

"This is a great tribute to the players," James told the *Swift Current Sun.* "It has been a lot of hard work to get this far. It has been a tough grind. There were times when it didn't look like we were going to make it."

The Broncos felt a huge sense of relief just to have made the playoffs. But when it came time to restart their engines, they just couldn't do it. The well finally had run dry. Emotionally, the Broncos were done.

At the time of the season when emotion means the most, the Broncos couldn't find it. The Prince Albert Raiders won the first-round best-of-five series in four games.

"Surviving the tragedy and all it encompassed and going on to make the playoffs, when we could have quit and gone home early, showed the gritty character that was part of each and every one of us," Wilkie says. "Although we eventually got beat in the first round, we felt pretty good about the season and how it turned out."

Game 4 of that series was played in Swift Current. The Broncos knew that a loss to the Raiders, who had finished third with a 43–26–3 record, would end their season, and the home team knew the odds were very much against them.

"It was a very emotional night," Wilkie remembers. "When the game ended, it was almost a relief that it was over. Finally, this season from hell was over."

The Raiders won that fourth game 7–4, and as it ended the 3,215 fans showed their appreciation with a thunderous standing ovation.

"The fans said it all," said an emotional John Rittinger, the team's governor. "That five-minute ovation told the entire story. They were saying, 'Thanks a lot, we're mighty proud of you.'"

It was hard to believe that what the Broncos had been through had really happened; that it wasn't a nightmare. But life, indeed, was moving on.

By season's end, the Broncos had purchased a new bus; well, a new "used" bus. It was a 1977 model MC8 that was purchased for $100,000 from Beaver Bus Lines of Winnipeg. It had a new motor and a rebuilt standard four-speed transmission with about two hundred thousand kilometres registered. It could seat forty-seven passengers on newly upholstered seats with overhead lights and a washroom in the rear. Unlike the old bus, there was no duct tape anywhere.

The "new" bus was mostly paid for through a fundraising dinner that had been sponsored by the Horseshoe Lodge and had featured Don Cherry as the guest speaker. Grapes even waived his normal fee for such engagements, "to help the Bronco hockey club." He thrilled the crowd of 285 as he spoke candidly and humorously about his days with the Boston Bruins and Colorado Rockies. When he spoke of the Broncos, he didn't hold anything back.

"If there was ever a team in the world who could have written off the season, this is it," he said. "It would have been so easy for them to quit, they've had a built-in excuse: losing four friends and teammates. But they didn't quit.

"It's an honour for me to be here and do what I can. I get chills thinking about how they made the playoffs through all this. They've got amazing character, which is something that can't be taught."

The NHL draft was held in Detroit in June. Four Broncos were drafted in the first two rounds. The Quebec Nordiques took Joe Sakic with the fifteenth selection of the first round. Six picks later, the Edmonton Oilers grabbed Peter Soberlak. In the second round, twenty-ninth overall, the Chicago Blackhawks took Ryan McGill. And with the forty-first pick, the Detroit Red Wings took Bob Wilkie. All told, five Broncos were drafted that day, as Ian Herbers was taken by the Buffalo Sabres in the tenth round.

As James would tell the *Sun*, "This is our finest hour. We have already lived the nightmare. Right now, we're living the dream."

CHAPTER 16

The 1989 Memorial Cup

As the 1988–89 WHL season began, the Swift Current Broncos' roster still included six key players who had been on their bus when it crashed on December 30, 1986.

Joe Sakic, the high-scoring centre, was only nineteen years of age, but already had moved on to the NHL's Quebec Nordiques. Other players, such as forward Tracy Egeland and defencemen Ryan McGill and Clarke Polglase, had been traded. Defenceman Ian Herbers had used up his junior eligibility the previous season and had left for the University of Alberta in Edmonton.

Some players — goaltender Pat Nogier and forward Lonnie Spink among them — simply had returned home knowing that hockey no longer was the most important thing in their lives.

However, goaltender Trevor Kruger, defencemen Danny Lambert and Bob Wilkie, and forwards Peter Soberlak, Tim Tisdale, and Sheldon Kennedy were back.

The Broncos also had added some promising young players, including four forwards with tremendous offensive skills: Kimbi Daniels, Peter Kasowski, Geoff Sanderson, and Brian Sakic, Joe's younger brother. As well, Trevor Kruger's twin brother, Darren, was on the roster. A defenceman with terrific offensive skills, he would get a lot of ice time and would run the power play.

The players knew that this team had the potential to do great things. And they expected to do well. As the season began, there was a real air of excitement in the dressing room.

The previous season, 1987–88, had been something of a success. The Broncos, coming off the season during which four teammates had died, went 44–26–2, for ninety points.

At first glance, that would seem to be a pretty good record. But it was only good for fourth spot in the eight-team East Division, behind the Saskatoon Blades (ninety-seven points), Medicine Hat Tigers (ninety-four), and Prince Albert Raiders (ninety-one). The Broncos beat the Regina Pats 3–1 in a best-of-five first-round playoff series, but then were beaten 4–2 by the Blades in a best-of-seven series.

Joe Sakic had tied for the WHL scoring title, but he was gone now and people were wondering how the Broncos would make up for having lost his incredible offensive and leadership skills.

The 1988–89 season started with a bang, especially for Tim Tisdale, a home-grown centre who was a quiet, unassuming guy off the ice. On the ice, however, it was a different story: he was a gifted scorer who let his stick do the talking. A back injury that required surgery had limited him to thirty-two games in 1987–88, but now he was back and he was healthy.

The *Swift Current Sun* reported that Tisdale, then twenty, was "playing the arsonist, burning the Regina Pats and Moose Jaw Warriors for ten points in two games as the Broncos opened the 1988–89 season with a pair of one-goal decisions."

Obviously, Tisdale was making up for lost time. Still, even he was surprised at his golden touch. "I knew I could go out and help the offence," he told the *Sun*, "but I never dreamed it would start like this. I'm shooting the puck better and more often. Last [season], I used to carry it a lot and always look for the open man. Now I am taking the shots. I think I've had fifteen in two games, and I had nine against Regina alone."

Tisdale also admitted that he had felt pressure the previous season, pressure that no longer was there. "There isn't as much pressure as last [season]," he explained. "That was my first year as a veteran and that's when I knew I had to be a leader."

Those two opening victories came on the road, and the Broncos didn't cool off. By mid-October, they had won eight straight games, the last one an 8–2 victory over the visiting Warriors. The Broncos won despite the fact that the team's general manager and head coach, Graham James, was kicked out after loudly criticizing the referee. In a bizarre twist, two players — Peter Soberlak and Dan Lambert — took over the coaching reins because assistant coach Lorne Frey was away on a brief vacation.

As it turned out, the game wasn't a whole lot about hockey as it included irate fans, thirty-two penalties, and one of the Broncos, Mark McFarlane — an eighteen-year-old right winger from Amherst, Nova Scotia — scaling the partition separating the two penalty boxes and clambering through the timekeeper's bench in an attempt to get at Moose Jaw defenceman Paul Giokas in the third period. As that went on, the scoreboard suddenly lost power.

Finally, in true WWE fashion, the always quotable James stated, "This was the worst display of officiating I have seen since Hulk Hogan lost his title. The refereeing was ridiculous!"

While the Broncos were getting plenty of offence from Tisdale, they weren't a one-man show. Trevor Kruger and Sheldon Kennedy were respectively named the East Division's goaltender and player of the month for October. Kruger had been in goal as the Broncos opened with twelve victories. He posted a 4.24 goals-against average — these were the days of firewagon hockey; the trap had yet to make its way into the WHL. Kennedy had a whopping thirty-three points in thirteen October games. He led the WHL in goals (twenty) and power-play goals (twelve).

Off the ice, the Broncos were enjoying solid fan support. Their average home attendance was 2,339, with a season-ticket base of 1,250, numbers that were rather impressive for such a small community. When Moose Jaw visited on Remembrance Day, the game drew a season-high 2,626 fans, perhaps because folks were looking for a WWE-type rematch.

"[The attendance] is up a little bit," James told the *Sun*, "but we had tremendous support all of last [season], too. We've had some good dates this year, the team has been winning, and we play an exciting style of hockey. The weather has also been good for our games so we've had a combination of a lot of things in our favour."

Sheldon Kennedy's speed often left him one on one with goaltenders.

James further stated that "the community seems to really take to this team and hopefully it will continue. I guess surprised isn't the word, because nothing surprises me, but we are very happy.

"I think it is the type of hockey we play, and we have a lot of players who the fans can identify with. That's something we try not to lose touch with in our scouting. It's good to have players like [Sheldon] Kennedy and [Dan] Lambert and hopefully we'll have a few more in the future."

The fans also loved the Broncos' spirit, which was never more in evidence than in a wild November matchup in Medicine Hat. The Broncos, who trailed 6–1 at one point, won 7–6 in overtime.

"It was unbelievable," Frey said. "You can't even imagine what it's like. It's impossible to comprehend what happened tonight. To be down 6–1 and totally out of it, then come back and win it — it's unbelievable."

During the game, with the Broncos struggling in the second period, James decided to keep the players at the bench for the second intermission. The players were forced to endure the Medicine Hat hecklers. "He was really disappointed at how we played in our first two periods. We were atrocious. The second was probably our worst period of hockey all year," Frey told the *Sun*.

By the time the Christmas break arrived, the Broncos had won twenty-eight of thirty-three games and were on a ten-game winning streak. After Christmas, the streak reached twelve before it was halted on New Year's Eve afternoon, when the Broncos were beaten 8–6 by the Tigers in Medicine Hat. The Broncos were without Soberlak (he had the flu), while Kennedy and Lambert were playing for Canada at the World Junior Championship in Alaska.

Tisdale had been unhappy with that performance and was determined to rebound in the rematch, which, as luck would have it, was scheduled for Swift Current on New Year's Day. He had two goals and four assists, and Wilkie had a shorthanded goal in the second period. The Broncos whipped the Tigers 8–2.

"We always seem to play well when we score the first goal," James told the *Sun*. "That was important, especially after we lost our last game. It gave us a psychological edge."

In the end, the Broncos won six of seven games without Kennedy and Lambert. "I wasn't surprised at all," Kennedy said upon his return. "I knew we had a lot of talent and I knew we were still capable of winning. We still had Tisdale, Kasowski, Wilkie, and Kruger, who are good hockey players, and … Kimbi Daniels and those guys came up big."

In December, the WHL had announced that James, for the second consecutive season, would be the East Division's head coach at the All-Star Game that would be played in Brandon on January 24. The head coaches came from the teams with the best record in each division after thirty-four games.

"I enjoyed my stint as [all-star] coach last year and I'm looking forward to it again this year," James told the *Sun*, also noting that there were "going to be some hurt feelings" when he announced which players would be going with him to the game. He certainly was right about that.

In mid-January, it was announced that five Broncos — Kennedy, Tisdale, Lambert, and the Kruger brothers, Darren and Trevor — would join James, Frey, and trainer Grant Farquhar on the East Division team.

W.H.L. All-Stars '88 Eastern Division

Front Row: Kevin Kaminski, Grant Tkachuk, Terry Yake, Joe Sakic, Kevin Todd, Todd Sceviour and Theoren Fleury
Middle Row: Graham James (Coach), Troy Kennedy, Richard Pilon, Dean Chynoweth, Brad Miller, Mark Janssens, Peter Soberlak, Craig Endean, Lorne Frey (Asst. Coach) and Gord Hahn (Trainer)
Back Row: Mike Modano, Mark Fitzpatrick, Scott McCrady, Jeff Ferguson, Bob Wilkie and Curtis Leschyshyn

The WHL's 1987–88 East Division all-star team. Note that the front and back rows are reversed in the caption on the photo.

The WHL's 1988–89 East Division all-star team.

Wilkie says he "was devastated not to have been selected." And, in reflection, he admits that he was by now starting to realize that James wasn't all he pretended to be. "Earlier in the season, Graham had told me he was going to recommend me for the Canadian team that would play at the World Junior Championship," Wilkie says. "Well, that didn't happen, so I was really upset when my name wasn't on the roster of the East Division all-star team, especially because Graham had hinted on many occasions that I would be there.

"This was typical of his behaviour and I now was beginning to see Graham James for the masterful manipulator that he truly was."

In their next game, the Broncos ambushed the Brandon Wheat Kings 9–5, and Kennedy, Kyle Reeves, and Wilkie set a WHL record by scoring three goals in sixteen seconds. That broke the record of seventeen seconds that had been shared by the 1967–68 Winnipeg Jets and the 1970–71 Saskatoon Blades. (It would later be broken by the Kelowna Rockets, who lowered it to twelve seconds on February 17, 1996.)

Wilkie learned on January 18 that he would play in the All-Star Game after all, as an injury-replacement for Brandon defenceman Kevin Cheveldayoff of the Wheat Kings (the same Kevin Cheveldayoff who is now the general manager of the NHL's Winnipeg Jets). The West Division won the game 5–1 before 2,933 fans. The game is mostly remembered for a hit by Tri-City Americans defenceman Steve Jaques on centre Mike Modano of the Prince Albert Raiders, who had been the first overall pick by the then–Minnesota North Stars in the 1988 NHL draft. Modano, a highly skilled centre who went on to a brilliant NHL career, emerged with a broken scaphoid, and at the time there was much concern shown for his condition.

And then it was back to Swift Current and on with the season....

By the time the Broncos left on their West Coast road swing at the end of January, they had all but clinched the East Division regular-season title. At the all-star break, they held a nineteen-point lead. Still, the Broncos didn't want to rest on their laurels.

"The biggest thing in these coast trips are the first couple of games," Frey stated. "From all past experiences, teams that have gotten off to good starts go on to have good road trips. If you struggle early, it

Courtesy of Bob Wilkie.

Bob Wilkie, a 1989 WHL East Division all-star.

seems to snowball the other way. But I think our guys are so confident in their ability that if that should happen they still have the talent to turn it around."

The trip began in Lethbridge on January 27, just three days after the All-Star Game. Then it was on to Kamloops; Victoria; Portland; Seattle;

Kennewick, Washington, the home of the Tri-City Americans; and Spokane. By the time it was over, the Broncos would have played seven games in ten days.

Things weren't entirely pleasant, either. The Broncos got whipped 9–2 in Kamloops. Prior to the start of the third period, James sent Lambert, Tisdale, Kennedy, Kasowski, and Wilkie to the showers.

While the Broncos finished with a 55–16–1 record, they won only two of the six games in the West Division. Wilkie missed most of those games with a shoulder injury that would cost him seven games.

As often happens to teams after long road trips, the Broncos struggled early upon their return. In fact, Prince Albert went into Swift Current and won 3–0 on February 12. It was the first time the Broncos, the highest-scoring team in the league, were shut out that season. James was so unhappy that he didn't speak to the players or the media after the game.

On February 24, the Broncos beat the visiting Portland Winter Hawks 7–4, clinching first place overall and home-ice advantage through the championship final, should they get that far.

The Broncos ended the regular season with one of the best records in WHL history: 55–16–1. They went 33–2–1 on home ice, establishing a WHL record for most victories at home, one that would be tied the next season by Kamloops and the Seattle Thunderbirds.

The Broncos had scored a WHL-high 447 goals, and five players finished with at least one hundred points: Tisdale (139), Kasowski (131), Kennedy (106), Lambert (102), and Brian Sakic (100). Darren Kruger and Wilkie, both defencemen like Lambert, finished with ninety-seven and eighty-five points, respectively. Trevor Kruger was among the top goaltenders with a 4.01 GAA and a 47–8–0 record.

The Broncos also were a hit at the box office. By season's end, they were drawing upwards of three thousand fans per game. In a community of slightly more than sixteen thousand people, they were drawing about one of every six Swift Current residents to games. To put that into perspective, that would be like the Toronto Maple Leafs, who play in a city of three million people, selling five hundred thousand tickets to every game.

With the playoffs approaching, those loyal fans were even more eager. On the day that playoff tickets went on sale, people started lining

Swift Current fans wait at the airport gate for the Broncos after the 1989 WHL championship series victory over the Portland Winter Hawks.

up at 4:30 a.m. The Broncos rewarded those fans by sweeping three best-of-seven series. That's right. They won twelve straight playoff games — sweeping Moose Jaw, Saskatoon, and Portland — to qualify for the Memorial Cup tournament, which was to take place in Saskatoon.

The Broncos wrapped up the WHL championship by beating the Winter Hawks 4–1 in Portland, and when their plane arrived back in Swift Current, they were greeted by hundreds of cheering, towel-waving fans. Parents, relatives, girlfriends, friends, and fans greeted them as they departed the TimeAir charter flight, hoisting the Msgr. Athol Murray Memorial Trophy.

But there still was this matter of the Memorial Cup.

With the tournament being held in Saskatoon, it meant that the Blades would be the host team. The Peterborough Petes were the Ontario Hockey League champions and the Laval Titans had won the Quebec Major Junior Hockey League championship.

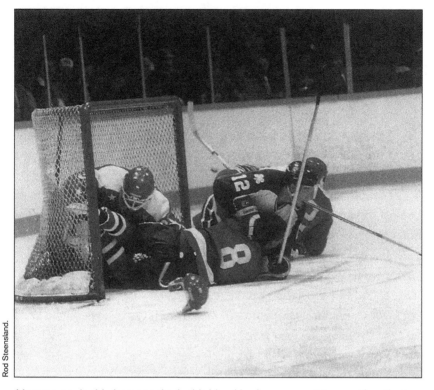

Rod Steensland.

Most teams, in this instance the Lethbridge Hurricanes, went to great lengths to stop Sheldon Kennedy (12).

Because the Broncos had taken only four games to oust Portland, they had a full week off. That allowed the Broncos to heal some bumps and bruises, and also to get settled down and focus on the task at hand.

"Since we had finished with the best record in the Canadian Hockey League," Wilkie says, "we weren't too worried about any of the other teams. We went into the tournament more concerned with our own play."

Their concerns were warranted, as they got off to something of a shaky start.

They had to come from behind to beat Peterborough 6–4 before 8,794 fans. Wilkie remembers that Kennedy "took a lot of abuse from the Petes — he obviously was a big part of their game plan, as they hit him at every opportunity. They really checked him hard and had him frustrated. On one occasion, he gave away the puck as he fanned on a clearance deep in our end, and it resulted in a goal by Peterborough's Tie Domi."

In the end, though, Kennedy scored two third-period goals to spark the comeback.

"I made a couple of mistakes I didn't know I could get back from. I just did my best to cover those mistakes up in the third period," Kennedy said.

In their second game, the Broncos again had to come from behind, this time to beat Laval 6–5 before 8,733 screaming fans. The *Sun* reported that the Broncos had played their "worst hockey in the playoffs" in that victory.

"This is the most relieved I have been in my three years in this league," James said. "Their goaltender [Ghislain Lefebvre] made some big saves throughout the game and I didn't think we were going to win."

The Broncos now had won fourteen straight post-season games and were looking at two days off before facing the Blades, a team they had swept from the second round of the WHL playoffs. The Broncos were feeling on edge, so they held a team meeting, the aim of which was to get everyone to relax.

"We also knew that a victory over the Blades would put us into the Memorial Cup final," Wilkie says.

Soberlak put it all in perspective when he told the *Sun*, "There has been a lot of pressure on us all year. We're used to it and we just take it all in stride. We all know we are going to have to play a lot better and make a better effort if we are going to beat Saskatoon. They have been playing well and we just have to dig deeper and do things that got us here.

"I'm looking forward to these next couple of games because they will likely be my last games in a Swift Current uniform. Hopefully, I can finish with a strong tournament and show the Edmonton Oilers brass who are here that I am capable of playing and, hopefully, they will make me a member of their club next season."

On May 10, there were about one thousand Broncos fans scattered among the SaskPlace crowd of 8,763. They proudly displayed their Swift

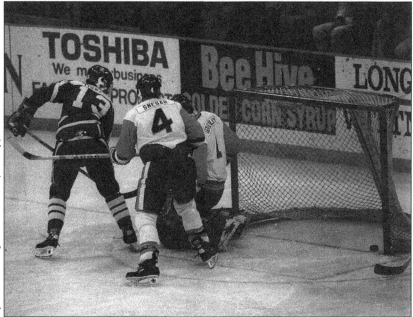

Tim Tisdale (13) of the Swift Current Broncos scored the overtime goal that won the 1989 Memorial Cup in Saskatoon.

Current pride by wearing Broncos sweaters, hats, pins, and anything else that was blue and green.

The Broncos disappointed their fans by losing 5–4, a decision that sent the Blades into the final and put Swift Current into a semifinal game against Peterborough, which had beaten Laval 5–4 in a tiebreaker. Finally finding their game, the Broncos beat the Petes 6–2 before 8,378 fans.

That set up the final. It would be played May 13, and would be on national television and in front of 9,078 frenzied fans.

"We weren't distracted," Wilkie says. "We knew this was our moment. The core guys who had been there from the beginning — Peter, Tim, Trevor, Sheldon, Danny, and myself — had no doubt we would win."

While they may not have had any doubts, the outcome was in doubt until the end. It turned out to be a classic junior hockey game, with the teams tied 3–3 after three periods.

The Broncos retreated to their dressing room after the third period and were awaiting the start of sudden-death overtime when

Tisdale, their oh-so-silent leader, suddenly stood up and declared, "I got it, boys."

"Yeah," Wilkie says, "Tizzy was talking about the winning goal."

Both teams came out fired up for the overtime, and there were close calls on both sides. The Blades had their chances, with Broncos goaltender Trevor Kruger forced to make five straight stops at one point.

But then, with the OT period slightly more than three minutes old, the puck came to Wilkie at the Blades' blue line. He made a series of moves that took him in behind the Saskatoon net.

"I was filled with so much energy and emotion that everything seemed to be moving in slow motion," he says. "Taking a look, I clearly saw my defence partner, Darren Kruger, standing all alone at the point. Without hesitation, I made a perfectly executed pass to him and Darren blasted the puck at goaltender Mike Greenlay.

"Tim Tisdale — who else? — was standing in front of the net for the screen, and he magically tipped the puck past Greenlay."

At 3:25 of the first sudden-death overtime period, the Swift Current Broncos became Memorial Cup champions.

"I was just standing there and it hit my stick," Tisdale said. "I still don't know how it went in."

The building was in a state of pandemonium. The Broncos threw sticks, equipment, and clothing everywhere.

Talk about a hometown hero.

Tim Tisdale had been born in Shaunavon, a farming community 108 kilometres southwest of Swift Current. However, he grew up in Swift Current and played minor hockey there. In 1986–87, he was a third-line centre who put up forty-nine points, including twenty-nine goals, in sixty-six games. The next season, he was limited to thirty-two games — and twenty-six points — by injuries.

So who could have seen the season he would have in 1988–89 when he finished with 139 points, including fifty-seven goals, in sixty-eight games? He continued that frenetic offensive pace in the playoffs, with thirty-two points, seventeen of them goals, in only twelve games. Then, of course, came the Memorial Cup–winning goal in overtime.

Rod Steensland.

Clockwise, from top left: The 1988–89 Broncos sign autographs during an on-ice session with young fans; a casual team photo; Sheldon Kennedy (left), Graham James, Lorne Frey, and Danny Lambert with the Memorial Cup; Tim Tisdale, who scored the winning goal in overtime in the 1989 Memorial Cup tournament, and Sheldon Kennedy enjoy the spoils of victory – a ride in a convertible during a parade.

Tisdale had been a twelfth-round selection by the Edmonton Oilers in the NHL's 1988 draft. He played three seasons with their AHL affiliate, the Cape Breton Oilers, before spending some time in Great Britain and more time in the ECHL.

He got his first taste of coaching as a player and assistant coach with the ECHL's Wheeling Thunderbirds in 1994–95, and by 1998–99 he was an assistant coach with the WHL's Regina Pats. Less than four months after signing in Regina, he found himself as the Pats' head coach following the firing of Parry Shockey. Tisdale stuck it out as the Pats' head coach through the 1999–2000 season, but then returned to Swift Current.

Looking for a more stable lifestyle, he began working at his in-laws' business, Wiens Agritec, an agricultural products supplier. He began as a bookkeeper, and now manages the business and has part ownership.

He has stayed involved in hockey through coaching and officiating in minor hockey and working on Broncos' radio broadcasts. He did a turn as president of the Swift Current Minor Hockey Association, and has been the referee association's liaison with SCMHA. In 2009, Tisdale was honoured as the Saskatchewan Hockey Association's coach of the year.

"I have coached at all levels … I have also worked with Hockey Canada on coaching manuals," Tisdale says. "I also do coaching clinics for the Saskatchewan Hockey Association." And through it all he treasures the memories of his days on the ice with the Broncos.

"Like most," he says, "I can say that the best experience of my life was junior hockey. The fact that I was able to play at home and have success makes it that much better. Living here, I realize more now than ever what winning the Memorial Cup meant to this community. I don't go a week without someone bringing up that game.

"You can always look back in hindsight and say, 'I wish this was different,' or 'I should have done this.' But at the time I had the pleasure of playing on one of the best WHL teams ever."

Twenty years later, Tisdale would tell writer Gare Joyce that something was missing from that championship Sunday.

"We took satisfaction for our accomplishments," Tisdale said, "but we just wished those four guys could have been a part of it. You're going to feel guilty somehow. And I still think a lot more about the accident than I do that championship and that goal."

As the enormity of Tisdale's game-winner hit home, the Broncos fans in attendance erupted and the players began celebrating. Wilkie, tears running down his cheeks, skated to Darren Kruger and grabbed him and hugged him. Peter Soberlak, Tim Tisdale, Sheldon Kennedy, and Danny Lambert were right there, too. They didn't say a thing; they just looked at each other.

Wilkie says, "The same thought was running through our minds: *We had accomplished what only a few years ago had seemed impossible.*"

Yes, they had done it. (On July 28, 2012, the team was among the inaugural inductees into the Saskatchewan Hockey Hall of Fame, which is located in the arena in Swift Current.)

Years later, Wilkie would write, "Together, we had done it, but we had not won this championship alone. We all felt the powerful spirit of the four fallen Broncos — Trent Kresse, Brent Ruff, Chris Mantyka, and Scott Kruger.

"Without a doubt, they were with us in Saskatoon that unforgettable day."

CHAPTER 17

The Coach Part 1

In the mid-1980s, the WHL was in the process of turning the corner, turning itself around from just another rough-and-tumble junior hockey league into a business with franchises that had million-dollar budgets and seven-figure price tags.

And before the Swift Current Broncos, who had recently moved home from Lethbridge, would take to the ice late in the summer of 1986, there were numerous decisions to be made, not the least of which were "Who would be the general manager?" and "Who would be the head coach?"

Ultimately, both duties fell to Graham James, a thirty-three-year-old former schoolteacher from Summerside, Prince Edward Island, who was a student of the English language.

"Graham was a tremendous find," John Rittinger, the man most responsible for bringing back the Broncos, said at the time. "I study the English language as a hobby. Graham has a degree in English literature. We try to trip each other up but Graham is never wrong." In other words, James was anything but your average North American junior hockey coach.

He had made something of a name for himself in Winnipeg minor hockey circles, where he had coached in the bantam and midget ranks.

While he had scouted for junior teams in Saskatoon, Flin Flon, and Winnipeg, he also had three years of junior A coaching experience in Winnipeg with the Fort Garry Blues, and had spent one season (1984–85) as head coach of the WHL's Moose Jaw Warriors.

(Theoren Fleury, then sixteen, would put up seventy-five points in seventy-one games with the Warriors. Sheldon Kennedy, then fifteen, played in sixteen games with the Warriors but didn't get even one point.)

James's coaching experience in Moose Jaw set him up well for the move to Swift Current. The Warriors had spent the first four years of their existence in Winnipeg, moving to Moose Jaw over the summer of 1984. So James, whose Warriors went 21–50–1, knew something about guiding a team through its first season in a new home. He knew all about what went into moving from one city to another and putting together a team.

What made James especially attractive to the Broncos' owners was the fact that he was a student of the free-flowing European style of hockey. That, James said, originated from a meeting with Bobby Hull, then a star with the World Hockey Association's Winnipeg Jets.

"I was trying to line up Bobby Hull for a charity hockey game [in Winnipeg]," James told Ed Willes of the *Regina Leader-Post* before the 1989 Memorial Cup tournament in Saskatoon. "He told me to get a couple of players and he'd bring a couple down. I met Hull at the Civic Centre in St. James around midnight. He had Anders Hedberg, Ulf Nilsson, and Lars-Erik Sjoberg with him."

Hedberg and Nilsson were Hull's linemates with the Jets, while Sjoberg, a defenceman, captained the WHA team. They were among the numerous Scandinavian players who would help put the Jets on hockey's map.

Willes reported, "James and his group, which included former NHL defenceman Kevin McCarthy, spent the next few nights scrimmaging with Hull and his new teammates. Actually, they spent the next few nights watching Hull, Hedberg, Nilsson, and Sjoberg create magic with the puck."

James told Willes: "I was twenty-one. They taught me another way to look at the game."

While in Winnipeg, James would spend many hours at the Winnipeg Arena watching the Jets go through their practice paces. It was while watching the free-flowing Jets that he came to believe that hockey played properly would be a game of puck possession. Broken down into its

1

T'was the game before Christmas and all through the place
The players were sitting with strange looks on their face*(s)*
The equip ment was hung by our trainer with care
And there wasn't the usual grease in his hair
He had everything ready - what an odd quirk
For the first time in months - he'd done some work
The Wranglers were in town for this pre-Christmas date
And with Nogier and Kruger, we knew we'd need eight
Except for Lackten, we took the ice as planned
He stayed behind to chip cement off his hand
The game started quickly and went end to end
And just when we were establishing a trend
Around Herbers they danced and went in to score
Eaton's could use him as a revolving door
Polglase could have stopped it but stood around like a fool
Like the rest of his people he just wanted to be cool
Lambert is build like a little fireplug
Darting here and there like a quick waterbug
With plays so fine and a shot like a luger
And willing to fight anyone smaller than Kruger
Proulx heads out with a grip like a vice
Too bad he plays like he's nailed to the ice
Smart, big and skilled Tizzy, has only one rap
Why does he play like he's having a nap
In practice 16 gets the defence in a funk
In the games however he looks not Sober but drunk
At the end of the second we're down by one
This team is used to being under the gun
Besides some contraption Lorne looks kinda mean
I'm leaving this place in my time machine
Back twenty year to the sixties it flies
For fun and adventure? - No I need some more ties!
Brosty comes in and yells about team pride
Ironic for someone just along for the ride
Back in the office I'm going over the roster
When in through the door comes old P.R. Foster

Poem written by Graham James for the 1986 Christmas banquet.

λ

I know we're still playing and I don't want a commotion
Can you cancel the third I've got a promotion
Mantyka starts the period with Greener and Spink
A fighter, a butcher and a missing link
Hustling and hitting - always on the go
Our own three stooges - Lonnie, Chrissy and Moe
Kruger's tripped on a break and boy is he hot
But the ref awards him a penalty shot
This is one of those times he isn't able to pass
So he really bears down and slaps it over the glass
Big Wilkie makes a rush - he has so much finesse
Too bad he plays like he's wearing a dress
Out of B.C. came a centre named Joe
With his goals and assists he helped the team's flow
His interviews too left people all numb
They couldn't believe he's that fucking dumb
Kresse plays two sports, he's quite an athlete
In baseball and hockey he's quick on his feet
One or the other though he'll have to call quits
I'd suggest hockey - at least in baseball he hits
McGill a tough guy, comes out like he's wired
He'll fight anybody now that Heeney's retired
No. 12's concentrating on hockey and school
With some time spent on acting the fool
He's often confused in the rink and in class
In hockey he won't shoot, in school he won't pass
On the end of the bench are Tracy and Hawk
Being young players they just sit there and gawk
If they don't overcome and calm their fears
They could be there for another three years
Sceviour's in the trainer's room, a place he is fonda
It's easier to find him there then it is fuckin' Honda
Despite all these bums, we'd come back to win
Thanks to the coach so handsome and thin
For the executive and fans we'd played outta sight
Merry Christmas to all and to all a good night!

simplest terms, it meant that if you had the puck, the other team didn't; therefore, you couldn't be scored upon.

James came to frown upon the dump-and-chase (a.k.a. chip-and-chase) game that had become so popular in North America. James wanted his team to play a puck-possession game. He didn't see much sense in giving up possession by dumping the puck into the other team's end and then having to go and try to get it back. Why do that, he wondered, when you already have possession?

Much like so many European teams, then, the Broncos weren't averse to circling back and regrouping should they reach an opponent's blue line and find the way into the offensive zone blocked. That, James came to believe, is the way the game is meant to be played.

Whereas the WHL had long been renowned for its rugged, oftentimes brawling, style, James preferred that his teams intimidate others with their power play. Take penalties against his teams and they would beat you with their power play. Over the 1988–89 regular season, the Broncos scored 180 power-play goals in 526 opportunities, an unheard of 34.2 percent success rate.

That isn't to say that James didn't understand the value of having an aircraft carrier on his roster. While the 1988–89 Broncos were winning with their power play, eighteen-year-old winger Mark McFarlane piled up 278 penalty minutes as he kept the flies off the team's five 100-point skaters — Tim Tisdale, Peter Kasowski, Sheldon Kennedy, Dan Lambert, and Brian Sakic. But McFarlane also could play: witness fifty-one points, including twenty-eight goals, in only fifty-eight games.

Having gone through the move from Winnipeg to Moose Jaw, James knew, too, that not all the players who had been with the Lethbridge Broncos would want to make the shift to Swift Current. And while the Broncos certainly provided hope for local youngsters who had dreams of playing in the WHL, their relocation muddied the waters for players who had been Lethbridge's property but who now belonged to Swift Current. Some would make the move from Lethbridge to Swift Current, while others requested trades and soon were on the move.

With help from the likes of super scouts Paul Charles and Bruce Franklin and assistant general manager and assistant coach Lorne Frey, James would get to work right away on shaping the roster that in the spring of 1989 would bring home the Memorial Cup to the smallest market in all of the Canadian Hockey League.

"What I liked about Graham as a coach was that he appreciated speed and finesse and hockey skill," said Peter Soberlak, a highly skilled forward who would join the Broncos in a trade from the Kamloops Blazers early in the 1986–87 season. "I played with Sheldon [Kennedy] and Joe [Sakic] and we had freedom to fly. We roamed and skated hard and made nice plays. Graham understood that. That was the way the game was changing to be successful. That was the hockey part I liked about him.

"What I hated about him was he was manipulative. He was volatile. He was angry. He used humiliation and degradation and sheer violence and fear toward young kids."

The angry, volatile side of James isn't one that was often in view of the public, although there were times when he would fly into a rage at the bench. Like the night of October 30, 1990, when the Broncos blew a 7–3 second-period lead and lost 9–8 to the visiting Medicine Hat Tigers.

The *Regina Leader-Post* reported that in the game's dying seconds, "James ran on to the ice and screamed at referee Kevin Muench. He charged the referee relentlessly and had to be restrained by Broncos players and both linesmen. He returned to the bench and threw sticks and water bottles on the ice. James then removed his jacket, tie, shirt, and a shoe before his players escorted him back to the dressing room."

Muench hit James with a gross misconduct, the same penalty James had received the previous season during a game against the Regina Pats. That night, James had said, "I don't like the term *gross misconduct*. It sounds like I pulled my pants down or something."

On this night, he had almost done just that. But this time, he wasn't talking to the media.

"I've never seen anything like it," one spectator told the Regina newspaper. "He just lost it. There are no words to describe it. After [the] game-winning goal, he just went nuts. He went out on to the ice and was charging Muench for about ten minutes. When he got back to the bench, he started taking his clothes off. The crowd started throwing paper and stuff on to the ice. It was almost like they were cheering him on. It was like in the movies."

A couple of days later, James was fined $2,000 and suspended for six games. "At least they didn't ask me for the shirt off my back," he said.

James was a huge sports fan who was especially enamoured with professional wrestling. After being disciplined by the WHL office, James referenced the NHL president, the commissioner of Major League Baseball, and what was then the World Wrestling Federation as he spoke with the *Leader-Post*.

"I was a little worried when you look at John Ziegler suspending Grant Fuhr for a year," James said. "Bart Giamatti suspended Pete Rose for life, and the big one was when [World Wrestling Federation president] Jack Tunney suspended Ravishing Rick Rude for a year after making comments about the Big Boss Man's mother.

"When I saw that on television I was concerned they might take their cue from that and I would be suspended indefinitely. In light of that, I came off okay."

That, in a nutshell, was James. He was bizarre, he was enigmatic, and he was tremendous with the press. He was an English major in university and he was a fan of professional wrestling.

And, as time would reveal, he was a whole lot more than all that.

CHAPTER 18

The Coach Part 2

Growing up in Winnipeg, Graham James played minor hockey at Sturgeon Creek Community Club, where he found himself on teams coached by John (Jack) Charles Nelson.

About a dozen years after James played there, three teenagers complained to police. Nelson was subsequently charged with and convicted of two counts of sexual abuse and one of indecent assault.

James has never spoken, at least not publicly, of any relationship he may have had with Nelson, who died in 1995. At this point, then, no one has any idea how much influence, if any, Nelson's lifestyle may have had on James.

James got his coaching start in Winnipeg, and was involved with community and Armed Forces teams, as well as bantam and midget clubs, in St. James. His stint with the bantam team ended in 1977 when, during a tournament in Minneapolis, he and some of his players were discovered playing video games in their hotel after curfew.

By the summer of 1983, James was ensconced as the head scout for the WHL's Winnipeg Warriors. They finished 1983–84 — their fourth season in the Manitoba capital — with an abysmal record (9–63) and promptly relocated to Moose Jaw. James made the move west with the

Warriors, but he didn't go as a scout. In the summer of 1984, James was named the Warriors' director of hockey operations and head coach.

Originally, Leon Devoin was the general manager; however, he resigned on August 10. Ten days later, the void was filled by Bryan Raymond, a Regina resident who went on to scout for the NHL's Columbus Blue Jackets for a few seasons. Raymond's stint in Moose Jaw was a short one — he was fired on October 21, and James added the title of acting general manager to his portfolio.

The Warriors went 21–50–1 in that first season and, by the summer of 1985, Barry Trapp was the general manager.

Trapp has an extensive hockey resumé, having later worked as Hockey Canada's head scout and the Toronto Maple Leafs' head amateur scout. He also has scouted for the Phoenix Coyotes. Trapp has said that James's relationship with the Warriors began to come apart in August of 1985. It was then when Trapp tried to arrange a meeting with James.

Trapp has said he called James, only to have the head coach tell him he was unavailable because he was going to Minneapolis with some friends to watch baseball's Minnesota Twins. When Trapp found out that the friends actually were junior hockey players, the general manager said he told the head coach that, in his opinion, that behaviour was inappropriate.

"I had no proof [of anything untoward]; only suspicions," said Trapp, who chose not to speak publicly on the issue until 1997, when he spoke with author Laura Robinson, who would write the book *Crossing the Line*. "My antennae went up that day. Something just didn't sit right with me.

"Graham didn't say, 'I'm going to Minnesota with a couple of our players.' As far as I'm concerned, he lied to me. Everybody had concerns, but until you have proof, it's hard to accuse a guy."

After finding out that James was travelling with players, Trapp approached the Warriors' board of directors — the Warriors are a community-owned franchise — and told its members that either he or James had to go.

The board chose to keep Trapp, who also took over as head coach and guided the Warriors to a 25–44–3 record. At the time, with Trapp choosing not to talk and James more than happy to, Trapp frequently was portrayed as a man who wanted to coach and thus had torpedoed James.

"I took a lot of heat for that," Trapp told Robinson. "And I never told anyone else why I really did what I did. I just kept telling everyone, 'It's in the best interests of the Moose Jaw hockey club.' I didn't want to be around the man. I wanted nothing to do with him."

In Winnipeg, James tried to laugh it all off by telling people he had been "Trapped."

No longer a WHL coach, James spent 1985–86 as head coach of the junior A Winnipeg South Blues of the Manitoba Junior Hockey League, while also scouting for the WHL's Kamloops Blazers. In fact, James had struck up a friendship with Kamloops head coach Ken Hitchcock and thought at the time that his immediate future in the game might well be with the Blazers. In the meantime, James and the Blues won the MJHL championship that season. They went on to lose the Western Canadian title to the Penticton, B.C., Knights.

By now, the Broncos were on the move from Lethbridge to Swift Current, and they were in need of a head coach. On May 1, 1986, James was introduced as their head coach. He would stay in Swift Current through 1993–94, when he left to help set up an expansion franchise — the Hitmen — in Calgary.

In eight seasons under James, the Broncos went 310–226–22 (.575). They experienced a bus accident in which four players died, and later won the Memorial Cup championship. They also got to the 1993 Memorial Cup tournament after going 49–21–2 in the 1992–93 regular season and 12–5 in the WHL playoffs.

They were, in a word, successful.

And everyone loved Graham James. He was named *The Hockey News'* Man of the Year for 1989, a year in which the Broncos had done the improbable and won the Memorial Cup.

But the award went to James for doing more than having guided a team to a national championship. In those days, he was championing the cause for goon-free, free-flow hockey. His coaching philosophy, he loved to tell people, had its roots in Winnipeg where, as a twenty-one-year-old coaching neophyte, he formed an association of sorts with a few players from the World Hockey Association's Winnipeg Jets.

It all began that late night/early morning when he and some friends played some shinny with some professionals at the St. James Civic Centre.

Bobby Hull, the Golden Jet, was the face of the WHA with the Winnipeg Jets. On this night, he brought with him linemates Anders Hedberg and Ulf Nilsson, along with defenceman Lars-Erik Sjoberg. Hull, Hedberg, and Nilsson were soon to be the talk of the hockey world for the free-flowing way in which they played the game.

Up until that point, James had been pretty much ensconced in the dump-and-chase game of junior hockey where, in order to be successful and sell tickets, you had to be able to beat up the other guy on the ice and in the alley. Or so the theory went.

A few nights of playing shinny with Hull and Co. changed the way James looked at the game.

In 1989, James was thirty-six and had surrounded himself with highly skilled players like Kimbi Daniels, Peter Kasowski, Sheldon Kennedy, Darren and Trevor Kruger, Dan Lambert, Brian Sakic, Peter Soberlak, and Bob Wilkie. God, they could play. Five players finished the regular season with at least one hundred points. Seven players, three of them defencemen, had at least eighty-five points. The Broncos scored a WHL-high 447 goals (only two teams scored more than three hundred in 2011–12), with a league-record 180 of those coming via the power play. That season, the Broncos scored those 180 power-play goals on 526 opportunities, an astonishing 34.2 percent success rate. (In 2011–12, two teams in the WHL didn't even score 180 goals in total in seventy-two regular-season games. Portland led the WHL in power-play goals with 108; Medicine Hat was next with eighty-seven.)

Knowing what we know now, it's easy for hockey people to look at everything that has happened and wonder how it was that they bought what James was selling. But in the late 1980s, James was swimming against the tide in terms of fighting and obstruction and all of the stuff that was so pervasive in hockey. And he was most persuasive.

"I lived in St. James for fifteen years but I'm not trying to be a saint or a martyr," James, an English major who never was at a loss for words, told Ed Willes of the *Regina Leader-Post* in a 1989 interview. "I'm just trying to provide a voice of reason. I'm not comfortable doing this. But I think we have a choice. Do we say what we believe or do we keep quiet so everyone in the league likes us? The easiest thing to do is remain neutral, but I don't think that's right."

James loved nothing better than to paraphrase Martin Luther King Jr., who once said, "The hottest place in Hell is reserved for those who remain neutral in times of great moral conflict."

James would put it this way: "The hottest place in Hell is reserved for those who, in times of moral crises, remain neutral."

The way he saw it, the game of hockey was facing a crisis, and he wasn't prepared to stay neutral. At the same time, however, the roster of the team that won the 1989 Memorial Cup included a winger named Mark McFarlane. He had fifty-one points, including twenty-eight goals, in fifty-eight games. He also had 278 penalty minutes. He was a great equalizer. His presence on the team was just one of many contradictions that surrounded Graham James.

"I went from Ken Hitchcock coaching all systems to Graham's coaching of no systems," said right winger Lonnie Spink, who was traded from Hitchcock's Kamloops Blazers to the Broncos in November 1986. Spink found it intriguing that players on the Broncos were allowed to be "as inventive as you wanted." And, as he pointed out, it actually worked, at least with this team, because the Broncos did win the 1989 Memorial Cup. By that time, however, Spink was no longer with the Broncos — he had exhausted his eligibility the previous season.

That freedom also extended to off-ice activities, at least with some players.

"I can't recall ever having more than a two-sentence conversation with that man," Spink said, adding that he and defencemen Ian Herbers and Gord Green, who were close friends, were pretty much left to themselves. "We were all older — nineteen or twenty— and he left us to ourselves, even having us phone curfew," Spink said.

This was in an era when there were a lot of initiation and hazing incidents that involved sports teams, and junior hockey teams in particular. While some coaches were of the opinion that such behaviour was good for team bonding, Spink found it interesting that James wasn't one of them.

"I had spent my rookie year [in Kamloops] loading the bus and helping the trainer," Spink said, adding that it was something of a shock to arrive in Swift Current and "see everyone treated as equals, even unproven rookies."

Ian Herbers (left) and Lonnie Spink.

In the end, and knowing what he knows now, Spink said, "I had no idea what was really going on and wish somehow I could have made a difference. Sheldon [Kennedy] and the people of Swift Current deserved better."

There also was the matter of James's temper. It's something that was never in evidence during his often lengthy conversations with the media. But it was there, especially in the Broncos' dressing room.

"Graham was famous for his temper," Spink said, "and I never knew a coach as volatile. We never had a dressing-room stereo for more than a month because he would get mad at practice, leave the ice, and beat our ghetto blaster with his stick."

Kurt Lackten, a grinding forward who was the Broncos' captain in 1986–87, didn't have any problem with James the coach. At the same time, however, Lackten recognized that manipulation was a big part of James's game plan.

"I thought he was a good coach. I got along really well with him," Lackten said. "I thought he knew the game well. As I got older and looked back at that, at the time I thought, 'This guy is really good with people.' Now I look back and I'm like, shit, no kidding. He has to be for his goals and why he wants to be good to people. You know what I mean?

"Looking back is hindsight, but I thought he knew people well. I thought he was really smart in the game. He could get a lot of response out of people. He was very manipulative but, of course ... he was a really smart guy in that regard. Unfortunately, he used it the wrong way."

And when "all that stuff came out ... I was totally shocked," Lackten continued. "I lived with Sheldon in Moose Jaw ... and I didn't know any of that stuff was going on. When it all came out, I was like, *What!* I was in disbelief. I couldn't believe it. *Really?*"

Barry Trapp, who had forced James out in Moose Jaw, believes he was, at the time, a lone voice in the wilderness. "When I was in Moose Jaw I never heard it come up," Trapp told Keith Bradford of the *Calgary Herald* late in 2009. "I was the first one that raised the flag. If anybody was aware of it or had suspicions, nobody came to me and told me."

Trapp isn't about to point fingers at anyone else, either. As he told Bradford, "Other people probably had suspicions, but nobody wanted to come out. [James] could have run for mayor. He was a media darling. He had people just completely fooled."

The facade, however, had cracked inside the Broncos' dressing room. Defenceman Bob Wilkie remembers early in 1987, when James bounced the team's stereo off the dressing-room wall.

"Looking back now, as an adult and after all that transpired from that moment on," Wilkie said, "I realize that what Graham James was missing was the ability to feel compassion for other people. Most of us were teenagers. We were lost and struggling as we tried to deal with a catastrophe that in many instances was the first time we had dealt with loss of life.

"Remember, too, that this wasn't a case of losing a distant aunt or uncle or a grandparent; we lost four of our best friends, teammates who dressed beside us, who went to war with us, who laughed and cried with us. Hell, some of us were still expecting the four of them to walk through the dressing room door, slip on their gear, and join us on the ice.

"So freaking out and berating us, bouncing a stereo off the wall, all because we had lost a hockey game, was totally inappropriate behaviour. I responded to his tantrum by turning away from him and turning him off."

Brian Costello, the *Swift Current Sun* sports writer who was on the Broncos' bus when it crashed, perhaps has described James better than anyone. "Graham was different ways with different people," he once said. "With reporters, he always had time to talk and always tried to help out. He was a very bright man and he was aware how the media could keep his image as an educator."

CHAPTER 19

The Coach Part 3

While some players may have recognized Graham James for what he turned out to be, none of them would speak out until well after Sheldon Kennedy went public with his accusations of sexual abuse.

No one was closer to James and to the Swift Current players than Gord Hahn, the veteran trainer. And yet, according to him, he was shocked when it all came crashing down. "I never saw it coming," he says. "I didn't see any warning signs at all, and I was around the team more than anybody."

Many of the former Broncos, Peter Soberlak among them, will tell you that James was a brilliant coach; that he understood the game, especially on offence, as well as, or better than, anyone. Others, like Bob Wilkie, gradually lost respect for James and prefer not to discuss that side of him.

"Without a doubt," Wilkie says, "Graham had developed a core group of talented players and that says a lot about his eye for talent. Unfortunately, it was the way he managed the team that made it rough for players like me. Graham was very blatant about who his favourites were and was extremely negative to the ones he did not care for personally … and that included me. I was constantly berated and belittled by him, and the three years I played for him seemed like ten years. I didn't want special treatment, but I did expect fair treatment.

"In every game, I would play a minimum of thirty minutes in all situations, and yet even after that I don't feel I got any respect from Graham. In my view, respect is a two-way street and I certainly did not extend to him any respect once I had been mistreated in this manner. Obviously, I do not have fond memories of Graham James."

Hahn, for one, understands both sides. "I agree with Peter. I agree with Bob in a way, but more so Peter," Hahn says. "The finesse and that that he had here as a coach ... he brought out the best in everybody, I thought. I think the players really respected him for that. And, yes, he was very smart."

After James was arrested and charged on November 22, 1996, Hahn says he couldn't believe the reaction around him. "It was wild," Hahn recalls. "I couldn't go to a restaurant, I couldn't go to work. The phone was ringing or somebody was calling.

"I went to Calgary and someone asked, 'What do you do?' I said, 'I work for the Broncos.' The response was, 'Oh, Graham James.'

"There were times when I actually got up and walked out of a place because I just couldn't take it."

Wilkie, meanwhile, says he wasn't surprised when the news came out that Sheldon Kennedy had accused Graham James of sexually assaulting him. "No, I wasn't surprised," he says. "I called Bob Harriman, my former billet, and we both found ourselves saying, 'I knew it.'"

During his time with the Broncos, Wilkie lived with Harriman, then an RCMP officer, his wife Janine, and their children. Now, more than twenty years after he played with the Broncos, Wilkie says he "had a feeling something was going on, but when you're young sometimes things just don't add up or click."

He also admits not knowing what good it would have done had he realized what was going on. "I was already on Graham's wrong side, and players who crossed him quickly got sent away," Wilkie says. "We were a group of teens away from home, living with strangers, riding a bus, and doing everything to pursue our dream of playing in the NHL. We needed a strong, well-balanced mentor, not a child-molesting, degrading, controlling monster.

"What people don't seem to realize is that we were compromised. Our youth was tainted, regardless of Graham's brilliant ability to spot talent, and he scarred all of us. We saw what was going on, but wouldn't allow ourselves to believe it could be true. To me, it is clear that Graham James was a master manipulator, and that's why he got such great results from his hockey teams. However, in the end, this same characteristic ultimately destroyed his life and others."

At the time of the bus accident and in the months afterward, little, if anything, was said or written about the fact that the Broncos players never were provided the option of counselling to help them deal with the deaths of four teammates. In the immediate aftermath, much was said about all that James had done to get his team through the wreckage of what followed.

Speaking at the memorial service after the accident, James had said, "You're alone and … at night it gets dark and you're in your bedroom and the show comes on over and over again, the same thing, and you can't get it to stop. I don't know if we'll ever shake that."

Years later, it became quite apparent that James was the reason why there wasn't professional counselling.

"The idea that Graham James got us through the bus crash is insulting," Kennedy would say later. "We didn't rally around him. The players rallied. He had nothing to do with it. And he kept the professional help from the team because he didn't want anyone to know he was a sexual predator — keeping out professional help was his idea, not the players'. The idea of keeping the dressing room door closed came from him."

Wilkie mostly remembers James as a manipulator. "Graham certainly had his favourites," Wilkie says. "He would call everyone when Shelly would go missing. He would have Shelly, Danny [Lambert], Kimbi [Daniels], and some others over to his house to watch movies on a regular basis. Some of us, as the outcasts or rebels, would joke about it, but later came to realize what a manipulator we had in control of our lives.

"He always was playing mind games with us. He gave no respect so we gave no respect. I remember Shelly and Danny screaming at him on the bench calling him a fat fuck and telling him to shut his mouth, what did we need him for … all of that kind of stuff.

"We knew what we had the ability to do and we did it. Not because of him but because we wanted it. He was not a motivator, unless you want to call getting everyone pissed at him motivating people."

Wilkie's relationship with James bothered the defenceman enough that there were times when he simply went home. "I did quit a few times," Wilkie says, "thinking, *What the hell am I doing this for?*"

But he always came back to chase the dream of an NHL career. And it's a career that Wilkie, who was drafted by the Detroit Red Wings in 1987, sometimes wonders if James didn't work to sabotage.

"Detroit used to come and see me play every so often and, always when we sat down, the reports from Graham got me in trouble," Wilkie recalls. "Was it all his fault? No, it wasn't. But he never stood up for any of the 'other guys.' If we were going to do anything, it was up to us. Most other coaches at that time were great at really helping their players. Graham helped who he liked, and left the ones he didn't like to fend for themselves."

Kennedy says, "There was fear. Graham holds that hammer over them. Power ... it's all about power. These guys are master manipulators. He loved the media attention."

And then there was the case of Ed Brost, who left the Broncos on his own during the 1986–87 season. Before leaving Swift Current, Brost gave his side of the story to local media, saying that his heart no longer was in it.

"I told Graham I'd be hurting the guys if I stayed," Brost told the *Swift Current Sun*'s Brian Costello at the time. "The simple reason is I wasn't happy. I decided this a long time ago. I wanted it to work out ... I really like Swift Current, the people. That's what kept me around for so long. I told Graham it's hard for me to leave. I almost started crying.

"Graham wasn't getting through to me. There was a barrier between us. I felt because I was an older player ... it seems he kind of pushes older players aside. I can't let that happen. This is my last year in the league. I have to prove myself elsewhere."

This wasn't the first time a player had left a team, nor would it be the last. This time, though, James, for whatever reason, chose to publicly address the issue. And he did so with guns blazing.

"We talked and it was clear he wanted to leave," James said. "We were going to let him part without any rancour. Everything seemed to be settled. When I heard what he said on the radio, I couldn't believe it. It's garbage.

"Every coach has players he knows better than others. If they don't admit so, they're lying. I treat all my players equal. I give them the same consideration and each receives the same reprimands for missing curfew, et cetera. I haven't talked to the players about it, but I invite you to ask anyone of them how they feel."

In the spring of 2001, twelve years after the Swift Current Broncos had won the Memorial Cup, and four years after Graham James was sentenced to jail, James was found to be living in Spain.

On January 2, 1997, James had pleaded guilty to sexually assaulting two players — Kennedy and one whose name was protected by a publication ban — on 350 occasions. James was sentenced to three and a half years in prison; he received day parole in 1998 and was fully paroled on July 1, 2000.

"The man who shook Canadian hockey to its core by committing more than 350 sexual acts on two teenaged players is back in the game and once again coaching," wrote Allan Maki of the *Globe and Mail* in the April 26, 2001, edition. It was a story that would earn Maki a National Newspaper Award nomination.

"Graham James ... has been coaching in Spain for several months. He was the assistant coach for the Spanish national team that recently placed second at the World C hockey championship in Majadahonda, Spain. The youngest player on the Spanish team just turned nineteen. Mr. James, forty-nine, also works as an instructor for coaches in the Spanish hockey system, where sources say he has no contact with players under the age of eighteen.

"Efforts to contact Mr. James were unsuccessful."

There was something of a firestorm at the time, especially considering that Hockey Canada had suspended James from coaching for life, but it died down within days, and James disappeared from the public eye.

That lasted until October 2009, when *Playing with Fire*, the biography of former NHL star Theoren Fleury, landed on bookshelves. Fleury had played for James-coached teams in Winnipeg and Moose Jaw. There long had been rumblings that perhaps Fleury had been one of James's victims.

In 1984–85, Fleury and Kennedy had been teammates with the Moose Jaw Warriors, who were coached by James.

"Theoren had to go to Graham's Wednesdays — Mondays and Wednesdays, I think," Kennedy says, "and I had to go Tuesdays and Thursdays. And we'd pass each other in the hallway sometimes."

In his book, Fleury claimed James had sexually assaulted him on numerous occasions, starting at the age of fourteen. In January 2010, Fleury filed an official complaint with the Winnipeg Police Service, prompting an investigation into James's activities.

James, however, was nowhere to be found until May 2010, when reporters from CBC News and the *Globe and Mail* found him living in Guadalajara, Mexico. James, who had lost considerable weight and barely resembled the five-foot-eleven, 235-pound Broncos coach, told CBC's Bob McKeown, "I'm impressed that you found me ... not that I've been hiding."

Asked to comment on Fleury's allegations, James replied, "Not a chance."

Unbeknownst to many people, James had applied to the National Parole Board for a pardon. It was granted on January 8, 2007, thus freeing him to leave his native Canada for Mexico.

The Canadian Press broke the story of James's pardon after being tipped off by Greg Gilhooly, a corporate lawyer who, it turns out, was another James accuser but at that point was protected by a publication ban.

That news was greeted with a national furor, which resulted in the federal government acting to tighten rules regarding the granting of pardons.

Eventually, James, sixty years of age at the time of publication, was hit with nine new charges involving three victims, one of whom was Fleury. One of the others, as came to light later, was Gilhooly.

James left Mexico in October 2010, after Winnipeg police issued an arrest warrant. He arrived at Pearson International Airport in Toronto and surrendered to police. In time, he was released on bail with conditions from the Headingley Correctional Centre, which is located just west of Winnipeg off the Trans-Canada Highway, and returned to Montreal. Among the conditions: a $10,000 cash bond, no unsupervised contact with anyone under eighteen years of age, no contact with alleged victims, and weekly check-ins with police. He also had to surrender his passport.

On December 7, 2011, appearing in a Winnipeg courtroom via video link from Montreal, James pleaded guilty to three of the nine sexual assault charges that had involved three players from 1970 to 1994. He entered guilty pleas to charges involving two of the players: Fleury and another ex-player whose name had been protected by a publication ban, but who turned out to be Todd Holt, another former WHL player who is a cousin to Fleury. Holt, a five-foot-seven, 160-pounder, had played in Swift Current for five seasons, from 1989 to 1994.

As part of the plea bargain, the allegations made by Gilhooly were stayed. At that point, Gilhooly stepped forward to tell his story, and the publication ban that had protected him was lifted.

On March 20, 2012, James was sentenced to two years in prison and was led in handcuffs from a Winnipeg courtroom to begin serving his sentence.

In sentencing James, Manitoba provincial court Judge Catherine Carlson noted that "there is no sentence this court can impose that will give back to Mr. Holt and Mr. Fleury that which was taken from them by Mr. James. The court expects there is no sentence it can impose that the victims, and indeed many members of the public, will find satisfactory."

She was correct.

"This sentence today is nothing short of a national travesty because we know that childhood abuse has reached epidemic proportions in our country," said Holt, reading from a statement in Cochrane, Alberta. "Graham James is laughing all the way back to the life he has always led, knowing that justice for him is but a blip on the radar."

The Crown had been asking for a sentence of six years; the defence asked for a conditional sentence as long as eighteen months but without jail time.

Kennedy was in the Winnipeg courtroom during the sentencing. Later, speaking outside the courthouse, he told reporters, "It's been a lifetime of working and rehabilitating with counsellors and two-hour sessions a week just to stay on track myself after the damage that Graham has inflicted, so to sit in there and hear that Graham James is rehabilitated really drives me nuts.

"Obviously, it's not a sentence we all want to see. At least he's going back to jail."

In handing down the sentence, Judge Carlson noted James had shown remorse and had apologized to his victims. She also pointed out that he chose to return voluntarily to Canada from Mexico, that he hadn't been in legal trouble since 1997, and that he chose to plead guilty.

"The two-year sentence is a penitentiary sentence," she said. "It acknowledges the seriousness of Mr. James's offences. It means sending back to jail someone who has not reoffended in the last fifteen years and has done all society has required of him during that time."

When the Crown announced in April that it would appeal the sentence, it was believed that James was being held at Stony Mountain Penitentiary in Manitoba. Should James apply for parole, he could be released from prison before Christmas 2012.

These days, the man who once was considered one of the best young coaches in the game of hockey certainly isn't remembered for that.

His brother Rusty summed it up best after Graham's first conviction in 1998: "I've been really upset, disappointed, and angry at this. I always thought he brought a lot of good things to the game, but now not a lot of that will be remembered."

After Graham was sentenced a second time, Rusty spoke publicly for the first time in fifteen years. "Throughout this latest process, I can't help but think of the Bernie Madoff case," he told Eric Francis of the *Calgary Sun*, referring to the infamous American fraudster who ran a massive Ponzi scheme. "Madoff is in jail for 150 years for stealing people's money. Graham stole much more than that from his victims — their childhoods, their lives, their dreams — and just got a few years.

"To me, Bernie's crimes pale in comparison."

CHAPTER 20

Leaving Swift Current

And just like that, it was over.

Sheldon Kennedy, Peter Soberlak, and Bob Wilkie were on their way back home.

The drive from Calgary had gotten them to Swift Current on Friday evening, shortly after the festivities to celebrate the twentieth anniversary of the team's 1989 Memorial Cup victory had started.

After arriving in Swift Current, the first thing they did was cruise some of their favourite haunts, and then it was over to their hotel. A quick change of clothes and it was on to a local Boston Pizza restaurant, where everyone was gathering as things got started.

There was, Wilkie admits, some apprehension at this point. "As we pulled into the parking lot of BP, we did a slow drive-by," Wilkie recalled. "Shelly and Sober both were saying, 'Fuck this. Let's get out of here.' I said we have to go in and Shelly reluctantly parked the truck.

"The tension was heavy as we strolled through the door, but as we started to recognize faces it lightened up quickly."

And then it was hugs and laughter all around and the stories started flying. Earlier, a replay of the 1989 Memorial Cup championship game in which the Broncos had beaten the host Saskatoon Blades 4–3 in overtime had been playing on the restaurant's television sets. (Of the players who were on the championship roster, only forwards Kyle Reeves, Brian Sakic, and Trevor Sim didn't attend the reunion.)

"We missed the [replay of the] game. We were the last three guys there," Soberlak said. "But it was great to be there."

Soberlak had treated the whole experience as though he were still playing junior hockey. "As usual," he explained, "any time we went on a road trip, the drive there and back is always the best part. Again, it was the best."

Looking back, Soberlak said he wasn't at all apprehensive before flying from his Kamloops home to Calgary, despite everything that had happened since the 1989 Memorial Cup. He admitted to a great deal of curiosity about what kind of welcome would await them in Swift Current.

"There wasn't any apprehension about being with the guys," Soberlak said. "When you're that close to someone, it doesn't matter if it's twenty or forty years, you never lose that. It took two seconds. As soon as I saw Bob in the airport it was like, boom, yesterday. And the same with Sheldon.

"You just know someone so well, especially when you spent three years together and go through what we went through."

As for travelling back to Swift Current, Soberlak said he "wasn't apprehensive … it was more curiosity, curiosity as to the response of the community. A little curiosity as to how people would react toward the event."

The morning after their arrival, Kennedy, Soberlak, and Wilkie went for another drive. And, lo and behold, there was Joe Sakic out for a run with his two dogs.

Sakic played two seasons with the Broncos, 1986 to 1988, but was with the NHL's Quebec Nordiques in 1988–89, when the Broncos won the Memorial Cup. Thus, he wasn't officially a part of the reunion festivities.

"Shelly, being the smartass he is, made a comment to Joe about his manly dogs," Wilkie said, with a laugh. "Who would have guessed in the middle of downtown Swift Current twenty years later we would be standing there as if nothing had changed.... We were standing around shooting the shit like nothing had happened, like we were eighteen again and coming back from summer break."

Holding the reunion and celebration with the 1989 Memorial Cup championship team was an idea that began in the Broncos' office, which at the time was under the charge of general manager and head coach Dean Chynoweth, one of the late Ed Chynoweth's two sons. Chynoweth and Elden Moberg, then the Broncos' assistant general manager, developed the idea and got the ball rolling.

Chynoweth, a rugged defenceman whose NHL career was short-circuited by injuries, left the Broncos' front office in order to join the New York Islanders as an assistant coach. During his WHL playing career, he had been on back-to-back Memorial Cup winners in Medicine Hat (1987 and 1988) and admits to being profoundly disappointed that "we have never had a reunion."

"I shared this with Elden and said these types of teams need to be honoured, not only for the players to get together and see what one another are doing these days, but, more importantly, for the fans, the billets, and the people who had enjoyed these teams.

"Alumni groups in junior hockey are very tough to get going, and you can imagine how tough it is in Swift with the Graham [James] era."

"I give them credit for doing it," Soberlak said of the reunion. But, in the next breath, he admitted that the spectre of Graham James was hanging over the festivities.

"But I still have apprehension — yeah, as to how I feel toward everyone involved back there," Soberlak explained. "Because there are question marks about who knew what and how things were dealt with, so there's always a part of me …

"The people and the community there are fantastic, but there are a few people within the hockey circles that, without mentioning names, I wouldn't, you know, I wouldn't have a lot of respect for … any respect, to be honest."

Asked if some of those people were at the banquet that was the centrepiece of the reunion celebration, Soberlak replied, "For sure. Front and centre."

Early on the day of the dinner, Kennedy, who had been a co-captain along with defenceman Dan Lambert on that 1988–89 team, was told that he would be asked to say a few words that evening. That turned out to be something Soberlak will always remember.

"The highlight for me was seeing Sheldon get up in front of that community and show the courage and the strength he did," Soberlak said. "He got up there and his speech was about the guys, about our team ... and the talent and the togetherness we felt as a team. He had an entertaining speech; it was funny. It blew me away — his courage and strength to do that."

By the time he arrived back in Swift Current, Kennedy's feelings had cooled. He was ready to walk into the banquet facility and look people in the eye.

"I don't have any bitterness," Kennedy said. "The way I look at that situation is that all you have to do is look at that town and look at their faces.... I'm sure glad that I have been able to deal with what I needed to deal with because, umm, there's a lot of pain left, there's a lot of pain in that town ... a lot of skeletons.

"I think the biggest thing is that you look at that situation and what we're trying to do is ... that situation didn't have to happen. People knew what was going on long before Graham got to Swift Current."

Leesa Culp also attended the reunion. Culp, who had been in the cab of a big rig that was directly behind the Broncos' bus, and who watched it crash, also was searching for some kind of closure.

What had been lost in the blur of time now had become a driving force in her life. As she watched the bus crash, she didn't realize that it belonged to the Broncos. Twenty years later, however, she felt a need to learn more about the boys — now men — who had been on that bus.

The Culps sat at a table with Peter Soberlak; Bob Wilkie; Joe and Debbie Sakic; Sheldon Kennedy; Sheldon's sister, Sherri, and her husband, Slawomir Borowiecki; and Sherri and Sheldon's mother, Shirley.

"At the end of the dinner, we just sat around and talked; they were reminiscing about the old days," Leesa says. "I was able to come to that dinner and sit at that table and find closure for me, too. That was really important. I felt like I could let the whole thing go at that point."

Culp admits that she was surprised — and thrilled — at the way she was welcomed at the reunion. "The reunion was an amazing thing to witness," she says. "I wasn't part of that team; I wasn't there all those

Pat Nogier and Leesa Culp at the Wellington West Bronco Golf Classic, July 2007.

years. But they never once made me feel like a stranger. I don't know if they felt like I was an intruder of some sort being there, but they never made me feel that way at all."

Culp also found it to be an emotional evening. "I got teary-eyed watching that video presentation," she says of the video that was shown on the televisions in Boston Pizza the previous night and was shown again at the dinner. "I knew what I had gone through ... even after all I'd discovered, I still couldn't imagine they got through what they did, and to get to where they've gotten as adults, husbands, and fathers."

To this day, the Broncos are a big part of her life. "I always think of the Broncos when I am dealing with something difficult," she says. "When I'm on one of my daily walks I wear my Broncos' hat. I also have a necklace given to me by Bill that has a four-leaf clover on it with the numbers of the boys engraved on the petals."

Wilkie remembers the ride home as being awfully quiet for the first hour.

"We each were wrapped up in our own thoughts," he said. "We had lost our innocence in Swift Current like many other sixteen-to-twenty-year-olds do at that time in their lives. Was ours any harsher? I think so — the accident, the presence of a child molester, the mental abuse that he gave to all of us.

"When love and compassion were needed, we got screaming and abuse. The people in charge who had known of his past seemed to overlook it, like it was not important or it would not happen there."

Soberlak looks back now and sees that James's abusing wasn't just sexual. "In institutions where there is a big element of power … Graham didn't just abuse Sheldon sexually, he abused his position of power in every way you can imagine, through everybody," Soberlak said. "Even the people who worked for him and he worked with … that was just his way.

"A lot of people don't understand that, but we understand that. Here's a forty-five-year-old man who's single and has to have sexual gratification somewhere, unless he's androgynous."

Soberlak was attending the University of British Columbia when Kennedy made headlines by speaking out about what he had gone through at James's hands. "It all made sense when I picked up the *Vancouver Sun*," Soberlak said.

With Swift Current in his rear-view mirror, Kennedy drove back to Calgary feeling like a free man. "I feel better than I've ever felt," he said, admitting that he has gotten rid of all of the anger that used to flow through his system like blood. He also has rediscovered the game of hockey.

"I actually go out and have fun playing … I'm having fun playing the game," Kennedy said. "I wish I could have played feeling this way, instead of … I can't describe the craziness. I never enjoyed the game from the first time this went on."

More than anything else, though, the return to Swift Current helped Kennedy become comfortable in his own skin. It helped reassure him that the new direction he had found in his life was the right one. At that point, he was well on his way to becoming a respected voice on the subject of the sexual abuse of children.

In the autumn of 2011, Penn State University was hit by just such a scandal. Kennedy, already a familiar face and voice in the Canadian media, was discovered by the media in the United States. He did numerous interviews and made a number of television appearances, including on CNN.

It was an appearance on CNN, he believes, that resulted in his being asked to travel to Washington, D.C., where, on December 13, 2011, Kennedy appeared before a U.S. Senate subcommittee on children and families.

With Kennedy's permission, here is the message he delivered:

> For many Canadians, hockey is everything. It is our passion, our culture, and our national pride. Like most boys growing up on the Prairies, I dreamed of playing in the National Hockey League, and luckily for me, that dream came true. I played for the Detroit Red Wings, the Boston Bruins, and the Calgary Flames.
>
> But it's not my dream that I'm best known for — it's my nightmare. As a junior hockey player, I suffered years of sexual abuse and harassment at the hands of my coach, Graham James.
>
> Despite the nature of the abuse, the hurt I experienced, and the fact I knew what was being done to me was wrong, it took me more than ten years to come forward to the authorities. Why didn't I say anything?
>
> This is the question that I asked myself again, and again, and again. It's the question I know everyone else was asking. And it's the question that plagues the millions of sexual abuse victims around the world.
>
> Even though I wrote a whole book on the subject, the answer is quite simple: because I didn't think anyone would believe me.
>
> In my case, my abuser was International Hockey Man of the Year! In Canada, that gave him almost god-like status. Sound familiar?
>
> The man who preyed on me took advantage of his position as a coach to look for children who were especially vulnerable — single-parent households, families with drinking problems, boys who needed a father figure, et cetera.
>
> These kids — and often their parents too — looked up to him as a hero. This was someone who

could make their dreams come true, and he used that trust to hurt them.

This imbalance of power and authority creates a deeper problem and it's the one that I think this subcommittee has to deal with head-on if you truly want to prevent child abuse.

In every case of child abuse — certainly in my own — there are people who had a "gut feeling" that something was wrong but didn't do anything about it.

Their attitude was "I don't want to get involved," "It's not my problem," "He couldn't possibly be doing that," or "The authorities will take care of it."

And that's what pedophiles and predators are counting on. They are counting on the public's ignorance or — worse yet — their indifference. That's what keeps child abusers in business. And that, Senators, is what you have to address.

From my experience, a child who is being abused has to tell — on average — seven people before their story is taken seriously. Seven! That is completely unacceptable.

When my story became public in 1997, there were people who refused to believe it. Many were angry that I had exposed an ugly side of their beloved sport.

Fortunately, Hockey Canada responded seriously to my situation and made abuse prevention education mandatory for their seventy thousand coaches. And this is the positive message that I want to leave you with this morning.

Seven years ago, I co-founded Respect Group Inc. in partnership with the Canadian Red Cross, internationally recognized experts in the prevention of child abuse.

Together, we launched an online training program for sport leaders called Respect in Sport. It focuses on educating all adult youth leaders on abuse, bullying, and harassment prevention, including a sound understanding of your legal and moral responsibilities.

Our belief at Respect Group is that we may never fully eliminate child abuse, but by empowering the ninety-nine percent of well-intentioned adults working with our youth, we can greatly reduce it.

I am proud to say that, through Respect in Sport, we have already certified over 150,000 youth leaders, which represents a high percentage of all Canadian coaches.

Many sport and youth-serving organizations have mandated the Respect in Sport program, and the list continues to grow: Hockey Canada, Gymnastics Canada, the entire province of Manitoba, school boards, and some early adopters here in the United States, including USA Triathlon and USRowing. In addition, organizations like Hockey Canada and Gymnastics Canada have implemented our Respect in Sport program designed specifically for parents.

We are also seeing proactive initiatives by the Canadian government to combat child maltreatment. Not just tougher legislation and minimum sentences for perpetrators, but a federal approach to prevention education that spans the multiple ministries that touch our most vulnerable: Canadian youth.

We have learned that social change takes time and has to occur at both the grassroots level and from the government on down. I am pleased to say that is exactly what is happening in Canada, and I hope it's what will happen here too.

Over the years, through my work at Respect Group, I've learned that

- educating the good people — the ninety-nine percent of our population — is our best defence to prevent abuse;
- training must be mandatory to ensure full compliance and reduce liability;
- the education has to be simple and consistent;

- all forms of abuse leave the same emotional scars, so training has to be comprehensive;
- education is best delivered online to ensure consistency, safety of the learner, convenience, and the greatest reach; and finally
- training must be ongoing, it's not a one-time thing.

Too often, society's response to child abuse is to focus on punishing the criminal. If the teacher, priest, or coach is sent to jail for a long time, then we feel that we've done our jobs as citizens or as politicians. Punishing the bad guys makes us feel good, but it does not fully solve the problem.

Senators, you need to give all adults working with youth, and all parents, the tools to recognize and respond to abuse when it first arises.

I am under no illusion that such an approach will fully eliminate child abuse, but I do know that mandatory education creates a platform within all organizations for that conversation to happen.

Empower the bystanders and you'll be taking an important first step in breaking the silence on child abuse.

Where Are They Now?

When the Swift Current Broncos' bus crashed on December 30, 1986, there were twenty-three people on board — seventeen players and six adults. Here's a look at what became of them.

The Adults

DAVE ARCHIBALD, the bus driver, was a huge hockey fan. With his mechanical expertise, he wound up driving the bus for the junior A team in Swift Current after the sale of the Broncos to Lethbridge in 1974. When the WHL franchise returned to Swift Current in 1986, he volunteered to drive the bus for the team and stayed through 1998–99. He later retired to the Turtle Lake, Saskatchewan, area with his wife, Kathryn, before moving to Lloydminster. They have a daughter, a son, two granddaughters, and a grandson.

Courtesy of Dave Archibald.

Dave Archibald, with wife, Kathryn.

Brian Costello, with wife, Terri.

BRIAN COSTELLO was the sports editor of the *Swift Current Sun*. He is now the senior special editions editor for *The Hockey News* and graciously provided the foreword to this book. He and his wife, Terri, live in Toronto.

JOHN FOSTER was the Broncos' volunteer director of public relations from the fall of 1986 through 1994. He retired from teaching in 2005 at the age of fifty-five. He and his wife, Joan, remain in Swift Current, although they travel to Texas during the winter months.

LORNE FREY was the assistant general manager and assistant coach with the Broncos. He is now the assistant general manager, head scout, and director of player personnel with the WHL's Kelowna Rockets, and is recognized as one of the top scouts in the major junior hockey world. He won a second Memorial Cup with the Rockets in 2004, and continues to bask in the glory of son-in-law Travis Moen's 2007 Stanley Cup victory with the Anaheim Ducks.

GRAHAM JAMES was the Broncos' general manager and head coach from 1986 to 1994. He resigned in 1994 to become part-owner, GM, and head coach of the expansion Calgary Hitmen. In 1996, James pleaded guilty to charges of sexual assault and was sentenced to three and a half years in prison. He was given a lifetime ban from coaching by Hockey Canada. James moved to Spain in 2000, where he was involved in coaching until 2003. He was found to be living in Guadalajara, Mexico, in the spring of 2010. In December 2011, he pleaded guilty to two more charges of sexual assault, and was sentenced in March 2012. At that time, he was living in the Montreal area.

DOUG LEAVINS was driving the Zamboni in the Swift Current Civic Centre in 1986 and filling in as the Broncos' trainer when needed. Immediately after Christmas 1986, trainer Gord Hahn was away with a Canadian team that was playing a touring Russian side, so Leavins was filling in for him when the bus crashed. Leavins later took the job as golf course superintendent at Chinook Golf Course, a Swift Current track. Leavins is married with two children. During the cold Saskatchewan winters, he enjoys downhill skiing and playing rec hockey. When the weather warms up, he plays a little golf.

The Players

ED BROST played two WHL seasons in Calgary before joining the Broncos in 1986. After four years in the WHL, he enrolled in the commerce program at Mount Royal College in Calgary, and then transferred to complete his studies at Alliance University College. He later attended the graduate School of Business at Queen's University. He

Courtesy of Ed Brost.

Ed Brost, with wife, Kim, and son, Jake.

and his family have now settled near Calgary. Brost and his wife, Kim, have one son, Jake. Brost is president of Trade Venture Development Group Inc., a professional services firm, and the chief operating officer at Acera Companies, which focuses on land development.

TRACY EGELAND was the second-youngest player on the 1986–87 Broncos; only Brent Ruff was younger. Egeland grew up on the family farm near Lethbridge and, during his minor hockey career, was coached by Randy Ruff, the younger brother of Buffalo Sabres' head coach Lindy Ruff. Egeland and Brent Ruff would become best friends. Egeland had a twelve-year pro career ended by a shoulder injury in December 2001. Tracy was the general manager and head coach of the Central league's Rocky Mountain Rage when the franchise folded after the 2008–09 season. The Rage played out of Bloomfield, Colorado. Tracy and his wife, Tara, and sons, Trent and Tyler, live in Artesia, New Mexico, where he works for Devon Energy.

Courtesy of Craig Finnestad.

Tracy (left), wife of Artie Feher, with daughters Jordan and Brenna, and Artie.

ARTIE FEHER, then a twenty-year-old goaltender, arrived in Swift Current after the 1986 Christmas break and was accompanying the Broncos for the first time when the bus crashed. He never did play for the Broncos, choosing instead to return to the SJHL's Nipawin Hawks after the accident. Feher went on to play one season at the University of Manitoba in Winnipeg and three seasons at Augustana University in Camrose, Alberta. He became a teacher and has worked in the Prince Albert area for a number of years, recently as an elementary school principal. He now is principal at Red Wing School, while also finding time to play hockey with the Kood-a-bins, a local rec team that was founded in 1994; he is an original member. He and his wife, Tracy, have two daughters, Jordan and Brenna.

Gord Green, with wife, Kim, and sons, Mike and David.

GORD GREEN, a hard-nosed defenceman, played with the Lethbridge Broncos in 1985–86 and moved to Swift Current with the franchise. Green left the Broncos in 1987, married Kim in 1988, and did a twenty-year stint as a combat engineer in the Canadian Armed Forces. He did six rotations overseas — Kuwait (1991), Croatia (1992), Bosnia (1994), Kosovo (1999), and Afghanistan (2004, 2006). The Greens live in Fort Saskatchewan, Alberta, where Gord is a power engineer at a refinery. They have two sons: David, a university student, and Mike, who plays junior A hockey.

IAN HERBERS, a hulking defenceman, began his WHL career in 1984–85 with the Kelowna Wings. When the Wings morphed into the Spokane Chiefs for 1985–86, Herbers found himself in Spokane. The Chiefs later traded him to the Lethbridge Broncos and he made the move to Swift Current when the franchise was sold. He would stay with the Broncos through 1987–88. Herbers was selected by the Buffalo Sabres in the NHL's 1987 draft but, rather than turn pro, he opted to continue playing hockey while attending the University of Alberta in Edmonton. He graduated with a degree in physical education, with an emphasis on coaching. Following his university career, Herbers played professionally and then got into coaching. In November 2011, he took over as head coach of the Milwaukee Admirals, who are the AHL affiliate of the NHL's Nashville Predators. On May 30, 2012, Herbers returned to his alma mater as the head coach of the University of Alberta Golden Bears. Herbers and his wife, Alina, have two daughters, Jessica and Nicole.

SHELDON KENNEDY went public in 1996 with his story of the abuse he was subjected to by Broncos GM and head coach Graham James. Kennedy since has become an advocate for survivors of abuse. In 2006, Kennedy published his autobiography, *Why I Didn't Say Anything*. Kennedy has co-founded a program — Respect in Sport — that has developed a grassroots tool to assist sport and community organizations in delivering on their commitment to create a safe environment for all participants. It provides online training that delivers abuse-prevention education. He travels throughout North America, always offering up solutions that will help protect children and young people from having to face what he went through. He lives near Calgary with his daughter, Ryan, who enjoys basketball and loves riding and caring for horses.

TREVOR KRUGER, a rookie goaltender in 1986, stayed with the Broncos through 1988–89 and then went on to a brief pro career. Currently living

Trevor Kruger (left), Pat Nogier, Bob Wilkie, and Darren Kruger at the third annual Wellington West Capital Bronco Golf Classic in Swift Current in July 2007.

in Lethbridge with his wife, Kristie, and their two children, Aidan and Payton, Trevor works as an associate director at Bluefox Association, a facility that provides support to adults and children with disabilities. When Trevor isn't spending time with his family or playing competitive hockey, he is busy golfing or lending his expertise to other young goalies through private coaching.

KURT LACKTEN, the captain of the Broncos in 1986–87, was born in Kamsack, Saskatchewan. He was drafted by the New York Islanders in 1985. He played professionally in minor leagues in North America and also played in Europe before trying his hand at coaching with the Broncos, Medicine Hat Tigers, and Red Deer Rebels. These days, he is a pilot with Hawaiian Airlines, flying Boeing 767s from Honolulu to international destinations, and trans-Pacific to mainland United States destinations. He and his wife, Julie, live in Queen Creek, Arizona, with their daughter, Kennedy.

Courtesy of Gord Green.

Kurt Lackten with daughter Kennedy on the flight deck of a Boeing 767.

Courtesy of Leesa Culp.

Pat Nogier and Bob Wilkie at the Wellington West Bronco Golf Classic in July 2007.

PAT NOGIER started his WHL career as a goaltender with the Kamloops Blazers, and appeared in the 1986 Memorial Cup before being traded to Swift Current. After playing with the Broncos for a season, Nogier returned to Saskatoon, where he became a city police officer. Nogier still is involved with hockey, working and coaching in the Saskatoon area. He also plays with the University of Saskatchewan alumni and the Saskatoon police teams. His wife, daughter, and son all play hockey. Their son, Nelson, a defenceman, was selected by the Saskatoon Blades in the WHL's 2011 bantam draft.

CLARKE POLGLASE was a rookie defenceman from Edmonton when he began his WHL career with the Broncos in 1986. After two seasons, he was traded to the Lethbridge Hurricanes. He went on to a lengthy pro career that included stops in the ECHL, IHL, AHL, and WCHL. He declined a request for an interview, writing, "Nothing personal. I wish you guys all the best with everything. Just a place I don't like to venture but something I will never forget."

JASON PROULX started his WHL career in 1985 with the Kamloops Blazers. A defenceman, he was traded to the Broncos in 1986. After the 1986–87 season, Proulx returned to his hometown of Fort Saskatchewan, Alberta, where he works at the Sherritt-Gordon nickel refinery.

JOE SAKIC began his WHL career with the Lethbridge Broncos, and was one of the players who wasn't interested in moving when the franchise was sold to Swift Current interests. But move he did, and he wound up being the WHL's rookie of the year for 1986–87. He went on to a Hall of Fame NHL career with the Quebec Nordiques/Colorado Avalanche. He retired as a player in 2009 and now works in the Avalanche front office as an executive advisor and alternate governor. He was named to the Hockey Hall of Fame in Toronto on June 26, 2012. Sakic and his wife, Debbie, who is from Swift Current, live in Colorado with their children, Mitchell and twins Chase and Kamryn. The Sakic family regularly returns to Swift Current to visit family.

Leesa Culp and Joe Sakic at the 2009 Swift Current Broncos Hall of Fame induction dinner honouring the 1989 Memorial Cup–winning team.

TODD SCEVIOUR began his WHL career with the Lethbridge Broncos in 1983 and made the move to Swift Current in 1986. After five complete WHL seasons, he went on to play for Team Canada under head coach Dave King. In 1995, after five years at the University of Calgary and having earned his first degree, Sceviour moved to Lenzerheide, Switzerland, to play and coach. His wife, Cheryl, played professional volleyball while in Switzerland. When they returned to Calgary, Sceviour went back to school to get a second degree, in education. He started out teaching at the elementary level and then settled into middle school. He has since started his own construction business. The Sceviours have two sons, Tyler and Ryan.

PETER SOBERLAK was born in Trail, British Columbia, and lived in Grand Forks, B.C., until 1979, when his family moved to Kamloops. Soberlak, then sixteen, spent one season with the Kamloops Blazers

Courtesy of Bob Wilkie.

Peter Soberlak (left), Sheldon Kennedy, and Bob Wilkie were together again on February 18, 2012, when the city of Swift Current held Sheldon Kennedy Day.

before being traded to Swift Current early in 1986–87. Soberlak was a first-round selection by the Edmonton Oilers in the NHL's 1987 draft and spent two-plus seasons with the Oilers' AHL affiliate, the Cape Breton Oilers, before retiring. He has a bachelor's degree in psychology from the University of British Columbia and a master's degree in sport and exercise psychology from Queen's University in Kingston. He is the chairperson of the physical education department at Thompson Rivers University in Kamloops, and also did a stint as president of the Kamloops Sports Council, an organization that oversees minor sports in the city. He also works with the WHL's Kelowna Rockets in the area of sports psychology. Soberlak and his wife, Amy, have one son, Jacob.

LONNIE SPINK joined the Kamloops Blazers in 1985. In late November 1986, Spink was dealt to Swift Current. After leaving the Broncos in 1988, Spink pursued a career as a respiratory therapist in Edmonton. He works in the adult ICU of the Royal Alexandra Hospital in Edmonton where he is "living and loving life." Spink and his wife, Trish, live on five acres just west of Edmonton near Spruce Grove. They have three daughters: Katelyn, Breanne, and Isabella. He still skates with friends from the WHL and school; he also trains and competes in half-Ironman triathlons.

Lonnie Spink with wife, Trish, and daughters Isabella, Breanne, and Katelyn.

TIM TISDALE was born in Shaunavon, Saskatchewan, but grew up in Swift Current. He began his WHL career with the Broncos in 1986 and ended it in 1989, when he scored the Memorial Cup–winning goal. He played nine seasons of professional hockey before moving into coaching. He returned to Swift Current in 2000 and now manages and has part-ownership in Wiens Agritec, his in-laws' business. Tisdale and his wife, Jenise, have two sons, Logan and Kyle. He has provided analysis on Broncos' radio broadcasts and is always involved in minor hockey. In 2009, he was saluted as the Saskatchewan Hockey Association's coach of the year.

BOB WILKIE grew up in Calgary and began his WHL career with the Hitmen before being traded to the Broncos in October 1986. He went on to a professional career that included NHL stints with the Detroit Red Wings and Philadelphia Flyers. He won an AHL championship with the Adirondack Red Wings and an IHL title with the Fort Wayne Komets. During a ten-year pro career, Wilkie played in the NHL, AHL, IHL, ECHL, and WCHL. Wilkie now resides near Calgary with his wife, Mikey, and children, Sadie and Cy.

The Broncos' trainer and two players weren't on the bus. Gord Hahn, the trainer, and defenceman Dan Lambert were in Winnipeg with an under-seventeen team that was playing against a Russian team. Defenceman Ryan McGill was ill, so he didn't make the trip to Regina.

GORD HAHN was a veteran trainer, a familiar face known as Hahnda in many rinks across the west. He joined the Broncos after working for the Victoria Cougars. He was working for the city of Swift Current and volunteering with the Broncos when they won the 1989 Memorial Cup. Hahn spent twenty-one years working for the City before retiring. He and his wife, Dianne, have one son, Tyler. They live in Swift Current where Gord is semi-retired, doing some work at a local golf course and helping out around the Credit Union iPlex when asked.

Danny Lambert, with wife, Melanie, and daughters Brook, Julia, and Melissa.

DANNY LAMBERT, from St. Malo, Manitoba, played defence for the Broncos from 1986 through 1990–91, when he joined the IHL's Fort Wayne Komets. Lambert was selected by the Quebec Nordiques in the NHL's 1989 draft and played twenty-nine games with them. He went on to play in various minor leagues before beginning a ten-year career in Germany in 1999. He now is an assistant coach with the WHL's Kelowna Rockets. He and wife Melanie have three daughters: Melissa, Julia, and Brook.

RYAN McGILL was a hard-nosed defenceman who had forty-eight points and 226 penalty minutes with the Broncos in 1986–87. Had the bus made it to Regina that night, he wouldn't have played because he was ill. Because the ensuing games were postponed, McGill was able to play all seventy-two games that season. He was traded to Medicine Hat before the 1987–88 season and won a Memorial Cup with the Tigers. After an eye injury ended his playing career, he got into coaching and was the head coach of the 2002 Memorial Cup–champion Kootenay Ice. He spent seven seasons as an AHL head coach and two as an assistant with the NHL's Calgary Flames. His contract wasn't renewed after the 2010–11 season. He was named head coach of the Ice again on July 4, 2012. McGill and his wife Karen have two daughters, Kate and Kyla.

Swift Current Broncos

1986–87 Regular Season

	GP	G	A	P	PM
F Joe Sakic	72	60	73	133	31
F Peter Soberlak (from Kamloops)	52	31	35	66	19
D Dan Lambert	68	13	53	66	95
F Sheldon Kennedy	49	23	41	64	43
F Todd Sceviour	72	28	31	59	52
F Trent Kresse	30	38	28	56	27
F Scott Kruger	36	19	37	56	32
F Tim Tisdale	66	20	29	49	25
D Bob Wilkie (from Calgary)	64	12	37	49	50
D Ryan McGill	72	12	36	48	226
F Kurt Lackten	65	20	20	40	97
F Warren Babe (to Kamloops)	16	8	12	20	19
F Erin Ginnell (from Regina)	29	13	6	19	6
D Clarke Polglase	69	2	13	15	33
D Ian Herbers	72	5	8	13	230

	GP	G	A	P	PM
F Rich Wiest (to Kamloops)	24	6	5	11	60
F Lonnie Spink (from Kamloops)	45	2	9	11	11
D Tim Logan (from Moose Jaw)	29	4	6	10	45
D Gord Green	57	4	3	7	189
F David Aldred	33	3	3	6	17
F Brent Ruff	33	3	3	6	2
D Ed Brost (to Brandon)	8	3	2	5	12
F Chris Mantyka	31	3	2	5	101
F Tracy Egeland	48	3	2	5	20
D Garth Lamb (from Victoria)	29	1	4	5	13
F Blair Atcheynum (from Saskatoon; to Moose Jaw)	5	2	1	3	0
D Paul Thompson (from Brandon; to Prince Albert)	12	1	2	3	34
F Terry Baustad (from Moose Jaw)	8	0	2	2	2
G Trevor Kruger	31	0	2	2	0
F Trent Kaese (to Calgary)	2	1	0	1	4
F Mark Stockham	2	1	0	1	2
D Jason Proulx (from Kamloops)	41	0	1	1	17
D Kevin Clayton	1	0	0	0	0
G Andres Froid	1	0	0	0	0
F Judson Innes (from Spokane; to Brandon)	1	0	0	0	0
D Terry Head	2	0	0	0	0
F Todd Oliphant (to Spokane)	3	0	0	0	0
G Gene Patterson	6	0	0	0	0
D Mike Wegleitner	7	0	0	0	12
G Mike Sutherland	9	0	0	0	2
G Pat Nogier	42	0	0	0	4

Goaltenders

	GP	MP	GA	GAA	S%	SO	W-L-T
Mike Sutherland	9	433	33	4.57	.851	0	4-3-0
Trevor Kruger	31	1,595	129	4.85	.854	0	13-13-1
Gene Patterson	6	250	21	5.04	.832	0	2-1-1
Pat Nogier	42	2,086	201	5.78	.847	0	9-23-2
Andres Froid	1	23	6	15.65	.727	0	0-0-0

1986–87 Playoffs

	GP	G	A	P	PM
F Tim Tisdale	4	1	4	5	2
D Bob Wilkie	4	1	3	4	2
F Sheldon Kennedy	4	0	3	3	4
F Todd Sceviour	4	0	3	3	0
D Ian Herbers	4	1	1	2	12
D Dan Lambert	4	1	1	2	9
F Lonnie Spink	4	1	1	2	12
F Tracy Egeland	4	1	1	2	0
D Gord Green	4	1	1	2	18
F Erin Ginnell	4	1	0	1	0
D Garth Lamb	4	1	0	1	4
D Ryan McGill	4	1	0	1	9
F Kurt Lackten	3	0	1	1	4
D Clarke Polglase	4	0	1	1	2
F Joe Sakic	4	0	1	1	0
D Tim Logan	4	0	0	0	7
F David Aldred	4	0	0	0	0
D Jason Proulx	4	0	0	0	0

Goaltenders

	GP	MP	GA	GAA	S%	SO	W-L
Trevor Kruger	4	240	19	4.75	.873	0	1-3

1988–89 Regular Season

	GP	G	A	P	PM
F Tim Tisdale	68	57	82	139	89
F Peter Kasowski	72	58	73	131	46
F Sheldon Kennedy	51	58	48	106	92
D Dan Lambert	57	25	77	102	158
F Brian Sakic	71	36	64	100	28
D Darren Kruger	71	10	87	97	72
D Bob Wilkie	62	18	67	85	89
F Kimbi Daniels	68	30	31	61	48
F Peter Soberlak	37	25	33	58	21
F Mark McFarlane	58	28	23	51	278
F Kyle Reeves	68	19	21	40	49
F Trevor Sim (from Regina)	42	16	19	35	69
F Blake Knox	70	13	17	30	116
F Geoff Sanderson	58	17	11	28	16
F Matt Ripley	40	9	14	23	25
D Kevin Knopp (from Seattle)	64	5	17	22	75
D Jeff Knight	65	4	12	16	74
D Wade Smith	63	5	10	15	126
D Joel Dyck (to Regina)	29	5	7	12	20
D Kevin Barrett	63	4	6	10	184
D Chris Larkin	41	3	3	6	37
G Trevor Kruger	59	0	4	4	20
D Jason Yuzda	17	0	3	3	6
F Jeff Denham (to Lethbridge)	5	1	1	2	2
F Jason White (to Seattle)	7	1	1	2	26
D Evan Marble	12	0	1	1	2
G Don Blishen	24	0	1	1	14
G Greg Reid	1	0	0	0	0
F Scott Albert	2	0	0	0	0
F Trent McCleary	3	0	0	0	0

Goaltenders

	GP	MP	GA	GAA	S%	SO	W-L-T
Greg Reid	1	2	0	0.00	1.000	0	0-0-0
Trevor Kruger	59	3,246	217	4.01	.865	1	47-8-0
Don Blishen	24	113	101	5.36	.845	0	8-8-1

1988–89 Playoffs

	GP	G	A	P	PM
F Tim Tisdale	12	17	15	32	22
D Dan Lambert	12	9	19	28	12
F Sheldon Kennedy	12	9	15	24	22
F Brian Sakic	12	9	9	18	8
F Trevor Sim	11	10	6	16	20
F Peter Soberlak	12	5	11	16	11
D Bob Wilkie	12	1	11	12	47
F Kimbi Daniels	12	6	6	12	12
D Darren Kruger	12	0	10	10	17
D Kevin Knopp	12	3	5	8	4
F Geoff Sanderson	12	3	5	8	6
F Mark McFarlane	7	4	3	7	39
F Peter Kasowski	7	3	4	7	5
F Blake Knox	12	2	1	3	30
F Kyle Reeves	9	2	1	3	15
G Trevor Kruger	12	0	3	3	2
D Jeff Knight	12	0	1	1	12
F Matt Ripley	4	0	1	1	12
D Wade Smith	11	0	0	0	21
D Kevin Barrett	12	0	0	0	4
D Chris Larkin	6	0	0	0	0
D Evan Marble	5	0	0	0	0
G Don Blishen	1	0	0	0	0

Goaltenders

	GP	MP	GA	GAA	S%	SO	W-L
Trevor Kruger	12	713	35	2.95	.908	0	12-0
Don Blishen	1	7	2	17.14	.750	0	0-0

1989 Memorial Cup

(at Saskatchewan Place, Saskatoon)
May 6: Swift Current (WHL) 6, Peterborough (OHL) 4
May 7: Swift Current 6, Laval (QMJHL) 5
May 10: Saskatoon (host) 5, Swift Current 4
May 12 (semifinal): Swift Current 6, Peterborough 2
May 13 (final): Swift Current 4, Saskatoon 3 (OT)

Sudden-Death Final

Swift Current 4, Saskatoon 3 (OT)

First Period

1. Swift Current, Kennedy (Lambert) 17:55
Penalties — Knopp SC (tripping) 2:43, Daniels SC (charging) 7:30, Holoien Sask (charging) 14:30, Kennedy SC (high-sticking) 15:35, Struch Sask (high-sticking) 18:22.

Second Period

2. Swift Current, Knox (Reeves, Lambert) 5:24
3. Saskatoon, Scissons (Struch, Sutton) 12:35
4. Saskatoon, Katelnikoff, 17:39 (sh)
5. Saskatoon, Kocur, 19:43
Penalties — Smart Sask (hooking) 1:18, Gerrits Sask, Kennedy SC (roughing) 9:34, Bauer Sask (hooking) 10:00, Sawtell Sask (interference) 15:52.

Third Period

6. Swift Current, Daniels (Kennedy) 5:59
Penalty — Lambert SC (hooking) 8:18.

Overtime

7. Swift Current, Tisdale (D. Kruger, Wilkie) 3:25
Penalties — None.

Shots on goal by

Saskatoon	10	13	10	1 – 34
Swift Current	6	6	7	5 – 24

Goal — Saskatoon: Mike Greenlay; Swift Current: Trevor Kruger.
Attendance — 9,078.

	GP	G	A	P	PM
Sheldon Kennedy	5	4	5	9	6
Dan Lambert	5	2	6	8	12
Tim Tisdale	5	5	2	7	4
Kimbi Daniels	5	5	1	6	8
Brian Sakic	5	2	3	5	0
Bob Wilkie	5	2	3	5	10
Trevor Sim	5	2	2	4	4
Peter Kasowski	5	1	3	4	0
Peter Soberlak	5	0	4	4	2
Kevin Knopp	5	1	2	3	6
Darren Kruger	5	0	3	3	2
Blake Knox	5	2	0	2	2
Jeff Knight	5	0	1	1	2
Mark McFarlane	5	0	1	1	6
Kyle Reeves	5	0	1	1	2
Geoff Sanderson	2	0	0	0	0
Chris Larkin	4	0	0	0	0
Wade Smith	4	0	0	0	6
Kevin Barrett	5	0	0	0	4

Goaltenders

	GP	MP	GA	GAA	SO
Trevor Kruger	5	303	19	3.75	0

Swift Current Broncos

Scott Albert, Kevin Barrett, Kimbi Daniels, Don Blishen, Peter Kasowski, Sheldon Kennedy, Jeff Knight, Kevin Knopp, Blake Knox, Darren Kruger, Trevor Kruger, Chris Larkin, Dan Lambert, Evan Marble, Trent McCleary, Mark McFarlane, Kyle Reeves, Matt Ripley, Brian Sakic, Geoff Sanderson, Trevor Sim, Wade Smith, Peter Soberlak, Tim Tisdale, Bob Wilkie.

Head coach — Graham James.

Award Winners

Most valuable player (Stafford Smythe Memorial Trophy): Dan Lambert, Swift Current.

Sportsmanship (George Parsons Trophy): Jamey Hicks, Peterborough.

Top goaltender (Hap Emms Memorial Trophy): Mike Greenlay, Saskatoon.

All-Star Team

Goal: Mike Greenlay, Saskatoon.

Defence: Dan Lambert, Swift Current; Ken Sutton, Saskatoon.

Centre: Tim Tisdale, Swift Current.

Left wing: Neil Carnes, Laval.

Right wing: Sheldon Kennedy, Swift Current.

(Sources: *www.hockeydb.com*, WHL)

Acknowledgements

There are so many people to thank for all they have done with the book and for helping me share this story with you.

First and foremost, I would like to thank Leesa Culp, who came into my life after twenty years and shared a passion to tell this story. If it weren't for her, you wouldn't be reading this; through the research, writing, editing, and constantly pushing forward, she has been an inspiration. The tough times she has gone through in the years that I have known her, and to be able to continue with such drive, is amazing. She is stronger than she knows.

Gregg Drinnan, for believing that this story was worth investing a part of his life in, was a godsend. Leesa and I knew we didn't have the experience necessary to complete this project. Through Leesa's tenacity, she was able to find Gregg who had been a part of the story as well. It is Gregg's expertise that made this book flow and become more than just a dream.

The Harrimans, Janine and Bob and their children, were such an important part of my life during the time I spent in Swift Current. I truly believe that had it not been for all of them, I wouldn't have been able to do the things that I have done. Bob was so insightful and wise; the conversations we had were deep and he shared an understanding that really allowed me to find the strength to move forward. (By the way, I am still really sorry about the toilet.) Janine was a big sister to me. I know that Janine helped me get in touch with my feelings, to actually feel as I was going through the loss and searching for answers. The love and support I received from the two of them was such a blessing. To the kids — Carrie, Suzie, and Patrick — it is because of you that I am the father I am today. You reminded me daily to stay in touch with my child side, to look at things from a different perspective, and to enjoy the simple things in life. I enjoy the cartoons with my kids now because of the times we spent watching *Pee-wee's Playhouse* on Saturday mornings. I love you all, and "thank you" really doesn't say how grateful I am for your allowing me to be a part of your family.

The Kruger household was a safe haven — unless we were losing, and then Fanner would give it to us. I spent a lot of time there with Darren and Trev, and it always was fun to sit and listen to the banter. We grew up in that house, either at the kitchen table or in the basement. Darren was my partner on the ice and off. His friendship meant a lot to me. I know that I was not always the best friend to him, and for that I am sorry, but the times we spent together were priceless, especially the Hawaii trip!

The great people of Swift Current supported us in difficult times, and that speaks volumes about the city's character. Winning the Memorial Cup was the greatest gift that we could have given back to a community that took us in and gave us what we needed in all aspects of life. In particular the MacBeans — Digger, Colleen, and Karen — were the people who provided stability in our lives. They were there with words of wisdom and compassion when we needed them the most.

To all of my teammates: it was a real pleasure to be a part of something so special. Before the accident, being an expansion team; after the accident, dealing with things we never thought we would have to, and then doing the impossible — winning the Memorial Cup. So many teams try and so few actually accomplish that goal. I think it says a lot about the character we developed together to be able to be called one of the best ever. There are records that we still hold.

My parents and brother provided constant support. They provided that solid foundation that allowed me to achieve my dreams. It was because of my family and the sacrifices they made for me that the doors of opportunity opened to me. Dad, you showed me strength; I watched how you dealt with the curveballs life threw at you and that inspired me. Mom, from the spirit you showed in venturing into the unknown time and time again, I learned that you must believe in yourself in order to succeed. And my brother — he gave the most. He gave up time with Dad because Dad was with me on my journey. His was the ultimate sacrifice, and never once did he complain about it.

And lastly, my family. Mikey, my wife, who has dealt with all of my ups and downs — this book really is for her. She supported and showed patience when most would have turned and run. Mikey, you have taught me what love really is. My kids, Sadie and Cy, have taught me daily to be a kid, to enjoy life even in the ups and downs.

I am sure that I missed someone, and there were so many who helped me along the way both before the accident and after. To all of you: thank you!

Bob Wilkie
Calgary, Alberta
January 2012

———

Deciding to write this book felt like the right thing to do from the first conversation I had with Bob Wilkie on February 20, 2007. Along the way I've had the help and support of so many people, and I'd like to mention a few.

Brian Costello has been a source of inspiration from my first email contact. He has generously provided guidance and been a source of encouragement and wisdom throughout the completion of this book.

Brian and Bob, you not only helped me tell this story, but you kept the lines of communication open so I could achieve closure in a part of my past with which I had never dealt.

To Thelma Kresse, Carter Kresse, Don Mantyka, Lindy Ruff, Darren Kruger, and Trevor Kruger, thank you for being gracious enough to speak with me upon request.

Dave Archibald, Ed Brost, Bob Crockett, Tracy Egeland, Artie

Feher, John Foster, Lorne Frey, Gord Green, Gord Hahn, Janine and Bob Harriman, Sheldon Kennedy, Kurt Lackten, Danny Lambert, Doug Leavins, Colleen MacBean, Pat Nogier, Todd Sceviour, Peter Soberlak, Lonnie Spink, and Tim Tisdale: thank you for sharing your memories with me and for allowing them to be used in this book. Thank you to Ian Herbers and Joe Sakic for allowing me the privilege to introduce myself.

Shelley Webber, Yvonne Scansen, Stuart McIver, Gordon McIver, Rae McIver, Murry Schock, and Calvin Plum: thank you for allowing me to share my adventures with you in this book.

I'd like to thank the Swift Current Broncos organization and the *Southwest Booster* for their support, the Saskatchewan Archives Board for giving me access to the *Swift Current Sun* issues that were required to complete this story, and the St. Catharines Public Library for having the facility to view them.

Bill Boyd, Richard Lapp, Kelly Putter, and Roy MacGregor: you gave me your time and writing expertise when I asked for it. Gregg Drinnan, you took our story and made it sing. A huge thank you to Arnold Gosewich, our literary agent, who found Dundurn Press, where there are people who believe this story is an important one and who wanted to publish it.

Rudy and Vicki Schindel, you have offered your kindness and generosity, and mostly a willingness to love me and my family for the misfits we can so often be. Leslie, I'd like to thank you for your help with my kids, your wonderful cooking, your ability to listen, and your warm fireplace, which has been such a source of comfort during some difficult times.

Mom and Dad, you've been my biggest cheerleaders since the first mention of this book. I am particularly relieved that I had a chance to share the manuscript early on with you both. Mom, losing you suddenly on December 21, 2008, has proved to be the hardest thing I've ever experienced. I was so looking forward to seeing your face light up when you saw this book for the very first time. I guess I wanted you to be proud of me. I miss you, Mom. Dad, I'm so thankful for your strength during this difficult time. You have suffered through your own losses, but somehow find a way to bring me comfort every time I speak to you. I love you, Dad.

To the rest of my family and friends, who I'm sure have gotten tired of my one-track mind over the last couple of years. I know that there have been times when I ate, drank, and dreamt the 1986–87 Swift Current Broncos, and your patience has been appreciated.

Leesa Culp
Beamsville, Ontario.
January 2012

———

For Dorothy, the love of my life and the most courageous person I have ever met. For Todd, who helps me maintain my sanity.

Thanks to Ian, for all of the help and the suggestions. And thanks to the good people of Swift Current, who experienced so much in such a short period of time.

Gregg Drinnan
Kamloops, British Columbia
January 2012

Resources

Interviews

Sheldon Kennedy (Leesa interviewed via telephone April 21, 2008; Gregg interviewed via phone and personally 2009, 2011)

Trevor Kruger (Leesa interviewed via email April 10, 2008, and received answers April 26, 2008)

Dan Lambert (Leesa interviewed via email April 10, 2008)

Peter Soberlak (Leesa interviewed via email April 8, 2008, and received answers April 15; Gregg interviewed April 18, 2008, as well as on multiple occasions in 2011)

Tim Tisdale (Leesa interviewed via email April 10, 2008, and received answers May 10, 2008)

Ed Brost (Leesa interviewed via telephone April 22, 2008)

Tracy Egeland (Leesa interviewed via telephone April 11, 2008; she sent a follow-up email the same day and received an answer April 11, 2008)

Artie Feher (Leesa interviewed via email April 10, 2008, received answers April 10, 2008, and received updated information January 2012)

Gord Green (Leesa interviewed via phone on November 5, 2007; she sent a follow-up email April 10, 2008, confirming the information)

Ian Herbers (Ian declined an interview; resources used were *www. hockeydb.com* and *www.johnstownchiefs.com*)

Darren Kruger (Leesa interviewed via email April 16, 2008)

Kurt Lackten (Leesa interviewed via telephone October 31, 2007; Gregg interviewed November 2011)

Ryan McGill (Ryan declined an interview; resources used were *www. hockeydb.com* and *www.flames.nhl.com*)

Pat Nogier (Leesa interviewed via email April 9, 2008)

Clarke Polglase (Clarke declined an interview; resources used were *www. hockeydb.com* and B. Costello, "Road to Recovery: 10 Years After Swift Current Tragedy," *The Hockey News*, December 27, 1996)

Jason Proulx (Jason declined an interview; resources used were *www. hockeydb.com* and Costello, "Road to Recovery")

Joe Sakic (Joe declined an interview)

Todd Sceviour (Leesa interviewed via telephone May 8, 2008)

Lonnie Spink (Leesa interviewed via email April 10, 2008, received answers May 3, 2008)

Dave Archibald (Leesa interviewed via telephone April 15, 2008)

Brian Costello (Leesa interviewed via telephone January 25, 2007)

Lorne Frey (Gregg interviewed September 27, 2008, and in 2009)

Gord Hahn (Gregg interviewed August 29, 2008, and in 2009)

Graham James (Graham was unavailable for interview)

Doug Leavins (Leesa interviewed via telephone April 10, 2008)

John Foster (Leesa interviewed via email April 21, 2008, and received answers April 26, 2008)

Colleen and Frank MacBean (Leesa interviewed via email May 3, 2008, and received answers May 16, 2008)

Bob Harriman (Leesa interviewed via email April 21, 2008, and received answers April 26, 2008)

Don Mantyka (Leesa interviewed via telephone May 7, 2008)

Bob Crockett (Leesa interviewed via telephone October 4, 2008, and in November 2011)

Bibliography

Chapter 3: The Broncos Come Home
"Swift Current." *Wikipedia*, accessed March 25, 2008, *en.wikipedia.org/wiki/swift_current*.

Chapter 6: Leesa's Ride
Mah, Steven. "Sombre Anniversary of Bus Crash Remembered." *Southwest Booster*, December 29, 2006.

McLaughlin, Tracy. "5th Teen Dead in Tragic Meaford Accident." *Toronto Sun*, January 23, 2007, *cnews.canoe.ca/CNEWS/Canada/2007/01/23/pf-3432014.html*.

Chapter 7: The Invisible Goaltenders
"Broncos Determined to Roll On." *Swift Current Sun*, January 5, 1987.

Chapter 8: Sober's Story
"Colleen MacBean Receives WHL Distinguished Service Award." Canadian Hockey League, March 7, 2006, *www.chl.ca*.

Kennedy, Sheldon, and James Grainger. *Why I Didn't Say Anything: The Sheldon Kennedy Story*. Toronto: Insomniac Press, 2006.

Kropf, Barret. "The End to End Beauty." In *Home Away from Home: A Tribute to the Real Heroes in the Game of Hockey*, 8. Saskatoon, SK: printed by author, 2006.

Chapter 9: Saying Goodbye
"K-man Explodes 4 Times in Broncos Comeback Win." *Swift Current Sun*, October 27, 1986.

"The 4 We Remember." *Swift Current Sun*, January 5, 1987.

"Thousands Attend Final Services." *Swift Current Sun*, January 5, 1987.

Chapter 13: Just an Ordinary Joe
Costello, Brian. "Road to Recovery: 10 Years After Swift Current Tragedy." *The Hockey News*, December 27, 1996.

Elicksen, Debbie. "Bus Ride from Hell." *Inside Professional Sports* (blog), February 17, 2007, *insideprofessionalsports.blogspot.com*.

Joyce, Gare. "Denial of Death." ESPN, April 10, 2007, *www.espn.com*.

MacGregor, Roy. "Lessons from Swift Current." *Globe and Mail*, February 2, 2008.

Wigge, Larry. "Sneaky Good: Joe Sakic Is all Action and No Talk." *The Sporting News*, January 14, 2002, 52.

Chapter 14: The Coroner's Report

"3 Not on Bus." *Swift Current Sun*, December 31, 1986.

"Coroner Releases Report on Dec. 30 Bronco Crash." *Swift Current Sun*, February 9, 1987.

"Inquest Called and Adjourned." *Swift Current Sun*, December 31, 1986.

"Survivors." *Swift Current Sun*, December 31, 1986.

Chapter 15: Back on the Ice

"47-Passenger Bus Bought by Broncos." *Swift Current Sun*, February 25, 1987.

"Body-Beaten Broncos Bury Blades Before Setback to Raiders." *Swift Current Sun*, January 26, 1987.

"Broncos Blitzed by Tigers Before Sellout Crowd." *Swift Current Sun*, January 14, 1987.

"Broncos Comeback Culminates Despite Season-Ending Setback." *Swift Current Sun*, March 30, 1987.

"Broncos Determined to Roll On." *Swift Current Sun*, January 7, 1987.

"Bronco Fans Cheer Team, Donations Mounting Up." *Swift Current Sun*, January 12, 1987.

"Broncos Return Friday." *Swift Current Sun*, January 7, 1987.

Costello, Brian. "Sports Probe." *Swift Current Sun*, January 12, 1987.

"Our Finest Hour, James Says of Team, Bus Fund." *Swift Current Sun*, March 16, 1987.

"Reception to Remember for Broncos on Friday." *Swift Current Sun*, January 12, 1987.

"Sharp-Shooting Broncos Rebound with Ideal Win." *Swift Current Sun*, March 9, 1987.

"'We're In!' Broncos Go Wild As Playoffs Clinched." *Swift Current Sun*, March 16, 1987.

Chapter 16: The 1989 Memorial Cup

"Broncos Ambush Brandon to Return Favour." *Swift Current Sun*, January 16, 1989.

"Broncos Begin Another Winning Streak." *Swift Current Sun*, January 3, 1989.

"Broncos End Road Trip with 2 Wins and 4 Losses." *Swift Current Sun*, February 6, 1989.

"Broncos Hit Road." *Swift Current Sun*, January 25, 1989.

"Broncos Shock Tigers." *Swift Current Sun*, November 23, 1988.

"Broncos Sweep WHL Final in Four Games." *Swift Current Sun*, May 1, 1989.

"Fans Enjoying Broncos' Success." *Swift Current Sun*, November 16, 1988.

"James Named All-Star Coach." *Swift Current Sun*, December 13, 1988.

"Kasowski Shines in Victory." *Swift Current Sun*, February 27, 1989.

Knutson, Darryl. "Broncomania Hits the Bridge City." *Swift Current Sun*, May 3, 1989.

_____. "Broncos Are Memorial Cup Champions." *Swift Current Sun*, May 15, 1989.

_____. "Broncos Two Victories Away from Memorial Cup." *Swift Current Sun*, April 24, 1989.

_____. "Broncos Win First Two Memorial Cup Games." *Swift Current Sun*, May 3, 1989.

_____. "Kennedy Recovers From Bad Start." *Swift Current Sun*, May 3, 1989.

_____. "Tisdale's Good Luck Leads Broncos in Game 4." *Swift Current Sun*, April 17, 1989.

_____. "Veterans Help Rookies Through Pressure Minefield." *Swift Current Sun*, May 10, 1989.

_____. "WHL Champions Receive Hero's Welcome." *Swift Current Sun*, May 1, 1989.

"Soberlak Coaches Team's Eighth Win." *Swift Current Sun*, October 10, 1988.

"Swift Current Dominates WHL Stats." *Swift Current Sun*, December 1988.

"Tisdale Leads Broncos." *Swift Current Sun*, October 3, 1988.

"Wilkie an All-Star." *Swift Current Sun*, January 18, 1989.

Yoos, Cameron. "Broncos Buried 9–2 by Blazers." *Swift Current Sun*, January 1989.

Yoos, Cameron. "Tisdale Scores OT Winner." *Swift Current Sun*, February 20, 1989.

Chapter 18: The Coach, Part 2

Robinson, Laura. "The Empty Net, Part Two." In *Crossing the Line: Violence and Sexual Assault in Canada's National Sport*. Toronto: McClelland & Stewart, 1998, 156–59.

Of Related Interest

Hat Trick
A Life in the Hockey Rink, Oil Patch and Community
Harley Hotchkiss
978-1-554884278
$36.00

In 2005, during the National Hockey League's year-long lockout of North American teams, Calgary Flames' co-founder Harley Hotchkiss — chair of the league — met alone with Trevor Linden, president of the NHL Players' Association. The wisdom and honesty of the team owner, many decades older, helped influence the popular young centre to convince fellow players to settle the dispute.

Harley has had that remarkable effect on people throughout his astonishing career in sports, business, and the community — a hat trick fulfilling his three goals in life. His absorbing memoir is an insider's guide to the development of North American hockey; the growth of the Canadian oil and gas industry witnessed by one of its most influential and individualistic entrepreneurs; and the behind-the-scenes story of enlightened philanthropy. Along the way, the Ontario tobacco-farmer's son tells of doing deals with the legendary Boone Pickens, going on safari with Swedish royalty, and becoming a partner with the mysterious Baron Carlo von Maffei.

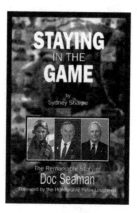

Staying in the Game
The Remarkable Story of Doc Seaman
Sydney Sharpe
978-1-550028812
$36.00

Peter C. Newman called him "the Totem of the Titans." From a small Prairie town, Daryl K. "Doc" Seaman became an icon of Canadian business and hockey. He is one of the last of a breed of postwar entrepreneurs and sportsmen who forged modern Canada, striking deals on a handshake and always keeping their word.

After flying eighty-two combat missions during the Second World War, Doc Seaman worked in the oil industry with his brothers, turning a small Alberta drilling business into a global giant, Bow Valley Industries. Later, he led a group that brought the Atlanta Flames to Calgary. Still a Flames co-owner, he helped reshape Hockey Canada and restore Canada's glory in international hockey.

Doc Seaman's life is a remarkable saga of courage, resolve, generosity, and success. It ultimately leaves us not only with a deep appreciation of one iconic Canadian but also with a wider understanding of our country.

Available at your favourite bookseller.

 **DUNDURN**
www.dundurn.com

Visit us at

Dundurn.com | Definingcanada.ca | @dundurnpress | Facebook.com/dundurnpress